An Ethnographic Study of Aruntatiyar of Tamil Nadu

An Ethnographic Study of Aruntatiyar of Tamil Nadu

Prof S. Seenivasan

Translated by

Prof Ajith Kanna

Foreworded by

Prof Y.S. Alone

KALPAZ

Published by

Kalpaz Publications
C-30, Satyawati Nagar,
Delhi – 110052
Ph.: 011-47034999, 9811692060
www.kalpazpublications.com
E-mail: kalpaz@hotmail.com

Distribution Network
gyanbooks.com
India, USA, Canada, UK, Australia, France

ISBN: 978-93-5722-376-8 (PB)

First Published, 2024

Printed at: Gyan Press, Delhi.

AN ETHNOGRAPHIC STUDY OF ARUNTATIYAR OF TAMIL NADU

Author: Prof S. Seenivasan
Translated by:, Prof Ajith Kanna

Contents

Dedicated to

My Lovely Daughter Mayakutti

&

My Life Partner Padhu

Foreword

Historical writings on ancient India right from the colonial times have always faced many difficulties. Broadly, the historical interpretations can be divided into few categories related with their applications or usage of the frameworks. It has its own historical trajectory of the development. Predominantly we observe the historical discourse can be classified into colonial/imperial discourse, Brahmanical discourse, Marxists discourse and the non-Brahmanical discourse. The other two that are added in the list is feminist and subaltern history. The colonial/imperial interpretation of history is centered around the white racial supremacy, the Brahmanical discourse is all about adherence to the varna-jati hierarchy together with the ideas of sacred and divine, the Marxist writings are based on the framework of classical ideas of base and superstructure whereas the non-Brahmanical discourse rejects the ideas associated with race, hegemonic religious ideas of divinity and sacredness as well as monogenesis religious views, the exclusive class reductionist method. Subaltern history writing has gripped many. It challenges meta-narrative of the historical writings. Its genesis lies in the conceptual formulations of great Italian philosopher Gramsci. Interestingly, the subaltern school of historians took seven long volumes to address the history associated with the scheduled caste and scheduled tribe population. Gramsci defined subalterns are the one who do not have access to power and resources and the Indian subaltern school of history failed to identify social groups/communities who fit in the definition. It may also be observed that Dr Ambedkar in his *Annihilation of Caste* observes that caste is not only a division of labour but also a division of labourers. The appellation of subaltern fails to address the tension, conflicts and hierarchies between the divisions of labourers.

The non-Brahmanic interpretation of history began with Mahatma Phule in the nineteenth century in Maharashtra whereas in Tamil Nadu, in the late nineteenth century by Pandit Ayothee Thass. Swami Dhrama Teertha, P L Narasu became the front runners of this model. Later it was Dr Ambedkar who became the biggest figure in using the non-Brahmanic framework to interpret the past as well as the present problems. The other figures that are noteworthy in this framework are Rahul Sanskrutayana, Anand Kauslyayan and later many others including Sharad Patil, etc. The book *An Ethnographic Study of Aruntatiyar of Tamil Nadu* by Prof S. Seenivasan is conceptualised in the non-Brahmanical interpretation of the past where the method of ethnography history is used to build the narrative of the community who are classified as scheduled caste in the present time. It is always a challenging task for a historian to write on specific communities as for the fact that the sources mainly the written or inscriptional are often absent. It may also be observed that there are Jati-Puranas available in certain areas of India that may help to reconstruct the history of the communities; however, they were written not by the community person but by the Brahmins of the areas who were employed to compose the narrative. Nevertheless, they become the important sources to understand certain historicity of the communities. It is also a fact that the historians would love to excavate the archive in a manner as if everything or every event of history is archived. Active selectivity also goes in the making of archive. Thus, creating limitations and over reliance on the archival repositories. On the other hand, the classical sources such as available literary evidence, numismatic and the inscriptional evidences are the body of the evidences which historians would like to all time relie to write historical annals. Prof Seenivasan has not only used linguistic, literary, inscriptional evidences to trace the history of the community but also used ethnography as important body of evidence to reconstruct the historical narrative of the community, in many ways, it's a challenging task.

Method of extensive filed work and survey is a laborious task that generates an archive of its own. Both the intrinsic and extrinsic problems associated with the body of material become an integral part of inquiry. The subjective context is emphasised to make the ethnography as reliable evidence in the process of writing community history. A mainstream historian or Brahmanical historian would find it difficult to accept such as a body of work that not only dwells into historical sociology but also the present-day conditionality. It opens many questions as well as problems with regard to the generic understanding of the terms and their implications and how normative readings have produced ghettoised meaning in reading and understanding of the available sources. The conflict of the land rights in the British Raj is a pointer to the fact that how communities constantly had to engage themselves all the time for their land holdings and historical oppressions, constantly having conflicts with the dominant communities who otherwise considered themselves as Dravida group, treating certain communities as that of 'others'. The othering process is understood with meticulous care by excavating the conflicts through the recent events as well as its historical characteristics. The book raises a very human question of how the Indian population by becoming a hierarchical varna-jati society completely lost the strength of introspections as well as humanitarian compassion that was part of the morality and ethicality functioned in the ancient Tamil society and its subsequent fragmentations. I am sure this book will enrich the non-Tamil speaking readers about the nature of Tamil Nadu in its historical transitions very briefly through the various methods employed in the reconstruction of the historical narratives.

Translation is a very difficult task and every translator tries to explore the similar words in the language he/she is translating into. Often one fails to come across the exact meaning in the other languages and may not capture the intrinsic value attached to a particular word. Tamil is among the ancient language in India that existed along with Pali. Its interaction with Pali is very pivotal and there are enough sources to understand the development of the Tamil language. Prof Ajit Kanna made some of those problems very clear and retained many words from Tamil as it is. It's a method that allows us to enhance our vocabulary and understand the punching nature that existed in Tamil language. I express my inability to understand Tamil, but the book in a translated form help in many ways to get familiar with Tamil terms and at times adjectives.

Prof Y.S. Alone

May 2023

JNU, New Delhi
Email: aloneys@yahoo.com

Note of the Source Book's Author

Two statements - Socrates's "Know thyself" and Ambedkar's "He who does not know his own history will not know any history" - can be considered appropriate for the people of the world. From the upper caste to the lower caste communities, they are keen to preserve their history through literature, legends, myths, inscriptions and oral histories. It is one of the most needed in today's times. In that way, it is our social duty and responsibility to bring out the historical importance, excellence and uniqueness of one's own society as it is without exaltation. This book *Tamiḻaka Aruntatiyar: Varalāṟum Vāḻvum* (An Ethnographic Study of Aruntatiyar of Tamil Nadu) is an expression of such social commitment and obligation.

Until 1922, the then government issued an order in the year 1922 to change the five castes, namely Cemmāṉ, Cakkili, Pakaṭai, Mātāri and Mātikā into a single name as 'Aruntatiyar'. In 2010, the then Tamil Nadu government issued an order to remove the name Cem'māṉ from that order and add the name 'Āti Āntirā' to the unified 'Aruntatiyar' after almost ninety years. It also announced a three percent internal reservation system as a result of this. Indeed, it is a decree that the entire Aruntatiyar community should celebrate and enjoy with gratitude. The micro-politics involved in the specific delisting and inclusion in these two government orders are also worth noting. Dictionaries indicate that the names 'Kuṟataṉ and 'Pātukaikkārar, which do not appear in the above two edicts, refer to Cakkiliyars.

The argument that Aruntatiyars, the original inhabitants of Tamil Nadu, are not Tamils, but Telugus, migrants, cobblers and manual scavengers has long been established among alternative communities. This book presents evidence that refutes this argument. Through these sources, this book is an attempt to bring to the attention of the Tamil community the proud and honourable past of the Aruntatiyar community, and it also brings to light the history of the enslavement of the natives of Tamil Nadu. Even historical and sociological studies have alienated the history of Aruntatiyar. While there are other Telugu-speaking communities living widely in Tamil Nadu, there is no intention to differentiate the Aruntatiyars as migrants and appeal to them. In fact, the Aruntatiyars belong to the Kuṟiñci land, one of the five land types of the ancient Tamils. On that basis, it is suspected that not only social injustice but also conspiracy has been perpetrated against the Aruntatiyars for a long time. We hope this book will clear these doubts.

The truth has to be made known to the people who cannot even digest the fact that Aruntatiyar is celebrated by the people of the community as a goddess (Goddess of Fire) who took her (Kuyili) own life to protect her own land by addressing Oṇṭivīraṉ who ruled Neṟkaṭṭāṉ Cevvayal Pāḷaiyam as local king and 'Cērvāraṉ', a social warrior who killed his wife's seven brothers who opposed their love at the behest of his romantic wife, as 'hero'. Hopefully this book has done that job.

Even though he has acquired the best degrees in education and traveled the whole universe, gained knowledge and experience through work, Aruntatiyar is left alone when he goes to his own village by a dominant caste school going boy calling him 'eh you Cakkiliyar man'. Cuppaṉ, a member of the Aruntatiyar Rescue Front in Sri Lanka, recorded his sentiments saying, "When someone says I'm a Cakkiliyan, I'm going to cry". Only those who have experienced it know its pain and suffering. Village children are brought up with untouchability imposed by mother's milk. This unhealthy disease has spread all over the villages of Tamil Nadu. This state of mind is not absent not only among the laity but also among some educated people.

In the 1980s, Aruntatiyar parents who wanted to name their son Māricāmi and couldn't enroll him in the school because "he doesn't deserve such name as 'cāmi (god), but if he wants, let him keep it as Māriyappaṉ. This is how the caste Hindu headmaster of a primary school in Nellai district registered this young boy's name in the school. During the same period, there were elders of the caste Hindus who were happy to name their beloved daughter as 'Rani' (Queen) and murmured to the parents of Aruntatiyar that 'how can a Cakkiliyar girl be named Rani?'. Director Mari Selvaraj's blockbuster film in Tamil 'Karṇaṉ' (2021) exposed the social misery of being denied the right to even name oneself. Healthy initiatives are needed to eradicate this entrenched disease. However, in the twenty-first century, among the younger generations of the rural dominant caste and Aruntatiyar, it is a bit comforting that they are getting used to the right to be related as young brother- elder brother, young sister- elder sister, grandfather-grandmother. If this healthy social practice continues forever, there is a chance of a healthy future society without caste differences.

Apart from this, the shameless social structure that makes only the Aruntatiyars do the social misery of 'human waste disposal' which is unrelated to them is painful. Even during the corona pandemic, this compulsion is still an ongoing story when alternative communities do not come forward to help. The government that will put an end to this act that the country needs to bow down to is the government that protects social justice. It will also become a state for the social liberation of Aruntatiyars. We hope that the Central and State Governments will create an environment that maintains the dignity of fellow human beings. At the same time, when there are thousands of professions in the world to survive, it is not understood why Aruntatiyars prefer to take up this vile profession. There are poor people among other upper caste communities living in Tamil Nadu. Under no circumstances do they volunteer to do the cleaning work. Our Aruntatiyar community should also be zealous not to indulge in this vile profession under any circumstances. It seems that there is no unity among the Aruntatiyars on this matter. There is a situation where a cleaner is looking for a successor job for his children. We can say that this is a setback for our social progress.

Take the Nadar (Nāṭār) community of Tamil Nadu. They were kept in the list of Scheduled Caste (SC) till 1917, which were considered to be polluted in two ways - (a) if you touch a Cakkiliyaṉ, you will be polluted and (b) if you see a Cāṉāṉ (another name for Nāṭār), you will be polluted. Gradual improvement in socio-economic status and the concessions brought by the Mandal Commission are now included in the Most Backward (MBC) list. If we want to mention a society as an example of the development and unity of an ethnic group society, it can be said to be Nadar (Nāṭār) community. I present a serious thought that like the Nadar community, our Aruntatiyar community should be united and strive to achieve development. The future should make one wonder if the Aruntatiyars were in the lower social class. That is the search for our social development.

In the recent past, there have been an abundance of incisive research books and essays on Aruntatiyar. These publications show that there is a need for these in the current Tamil society. In that way, the book *An Ethnographic Study of Aruntatiyars of Tamil Nadu* has been written with an ethnographic approach to the social history and life of Aruntatiyars.

With the financial support of the University Grants Commission (UGC), the field study entitled *An Ethnographic Study of Dalit Folk Ballads of Southern Tamil Nadu* enabled the collection of completely unpublished Aruntatiyars' ballads. They were also published under the title *Dalit Folk Ballads* (2010). As part of the chapter of the book's references, I had to write a research introduction on the history of Aruntatiyar. It is the extension of that conversation that laid the foundation for the creation of this study.

This book consists of eight chapters. The first chapter explains the history and definitions of ethnography as a preview to the course of this study on Aruntatiyar ethnohistory. It also lists the need and benefits of ethnography in Indian and Tamil Nadu context. In the context of modern literatures being ethnographically viewed, this chapter presents a research methodology that suppresses folk literature types of narratives within the ethnographic framework and restores ethnohistory in a folk dialectic way. Thus, it brings to the attention of the Tamil community the previously unpublished Aruntatiyar ballads collected through field research.

The second chapter deals with the nature of written histories. It also proposes that the Aruntatiyars, the original inhabitants, should write history from the subaltern perspective. This chapter also describes in detail the Vedic and spiritual histories and it records the Buddhist and Shaivite traditions of Aruntatiyars.

The third chapter reveals the rare history of the Aruntatiyars through oral history, literature, stone inscriptions, copperplate inscriptions and written history. Social thinker and writer Mr Mathivannan's writings greatly helped shape this particular chapter.

The fourth chapter introduces the unknown Pāḷaiyams of Aruntatiyars and it focuses largely on the ethnohistory of Neṟkaṭṭāṉ Cevvayal Pāḷaiyam and Āvuṭaiyār Pāḷaiyam.

The fifth chapter describes the role of Oṇṭivīraṉ in the Indian freedom struggle. Folk narratives and oral history is constructed through folk ballads of Oṇṭivīraṉ of Neṟkaṭṭāṉ Cevvayal as son of the soil.

The sixth chapter identifies that, not only in the Aruntatiyar community but also among other communities, there were famous warriors named Oṇṭivīraṉ, other Oṇṭivīraṉs, Kuyili, and others. At a time when Oṇṭivīraṉ's popularity has reached its peak in history, the fact that alternative groups are trying to claim it, indicates that Aruntatiyar should be bit cautious.

The seventh chapter discusses the unknown local deities of Aruntatiyar clan and explains that honour killings have started not only in modern times but also a few centuries ago. This chapter establishes the presence of Aruntatiyar deities as powerful deity through the murder confessions.

The final chapter narrates the history of Kuyili, a warrior woman of the Aruntatiyar clan, as a history of resurgent Dalit feminism. This chapter describes how the heroic and wise Aruntatiyar woman's life of sacrifice transformed into a goddess of worship and as a fire-breathing goddess.

I am grateful to Dr L. Murugan (Former Vice Chairman, National SC Commission) for having given me valuable suggestions and encouragement to complete this book.

I am also thankful to Dr S.Manokaran (DGM, SIPCOT, Rtd) for having given me an idea to use WhatsApp platform to send my book for The Best Writers' Award announced by Government of Tamil Nadu.

On the whole, I would like to humbly place on record that this book has touched the socio-cultural history and life of Tamil Nadu's Aruntatiyars to some extent.

I am extremely thankful and grateful to the Adi Dravidar Welfare Department of the Tamil Nadu Government for identifying the best Adi Dravidar writers and recognizing and rewarding their writings in the name of best work. During the Covid-19 pandemic, the awardees were invited to Chennai and in an environment where it was not possible to present the award and sent the certificate of appreciation and the cheque for the incentive to Delhi, where I am working. My heartfelt thanks to Mr Muniyanathan, Commissioner of Adi Dravidar Welfare Department, who took prompt action to provide it through Principal Resident Commissioner, Tamil Nadu House, New Delhi. Mr Durairaj who works in the Adi Dravidar Welfare Department, contacted me and exchanged information on this matter. Thank you very much to Mr Durairaj.

The Principal Resident Commissioner Mr Hitesh Kumar Makwana, IAS at New Delhi who formally presented a certificate of appreciation and a cheque for incentives without delay in accepting the prompt action of the Tamil Nadu government. Many thanks to Mr Hitesh Kumar Makwana for his kind gesture. I am eternally grateful to Mr Santhanam Ayyangar, Consultant, Sri Venkateswara College, New Delhi, who came and helped me on behalf of my college on the day of the award.

Friends who studied and worked with O. Muthaiah and Siva. Vivekananthan, who did not hesitate to give a greeting from a new angle when he was rightly asked for a greeting, is a credit to this book.

Sincere thanks and gratitude to the former principal Dr Mrs Hemalatha Reddy and the present principal of Sri Venkateswara College Prof Mrs C. Sheela Reddy who have created a working environment conducive to teaching and creative research.

I am extremely grateful to my beloved parents Mr M. Sappani and Mrs S. Kanthari who have brought me up to this level. My gratitude goes to my maternal uncle Mr S. Palavesam, Superintendent (Retd), SBCO, Indian Postal Services, who has provided me with the financial assistance to my education and helped me travel smoothly in my academic journey. I am also thankful to my sisters and brothers who have enormously, along with my parents, helped me to complete my education successfully.

I am also grateful to my beloved wife N. Kalithasammal, who has given me full freedom to write books and who has read the books written in full and carefully identified and pointed out the fine flaws.

Many thanks to Dr Suresh K (Guest Lecturer, Delhi School of Journalism, University of Delhi and Sri Venkateswara College, University of Delhi) for proofreading the typed and printed materials. He has done the diacritic work of Tamil references.

Sankarankovil Vijayaragavan is also believed to be the one who provided the necessary source materials during this journey of writing of my book, collected data and sent them to Delhi tirelessly to conduct field research on the Aruntatiyar local deities.

Balaji International Publishers, New Delhi is boldly publishing this book on Ethnography as its maiden venture. Thanks to the efforts and courage of the publisher.

Mrs K.L. Lakshmi, who has helped with page layout for my other books, has also helped with this book. Many thanks to my friend Kavi Pāskar who helped me by beautifully designing the cover of the book. Also, a big thank you to Mr Nityanandam, owner of Neytal Patippakam) and all those who have loved and helped in many ways during the creation of this book. Many thanks to them.

Heartfelt thanks to Mr M.A. Krishnamurthy for his constant communication and encouragement from the day of applying for the award till the time of receiving the award. As soon as I got the news of receiving the award from the Tamil Nadu government, the entire Tamil Nadu Aruntatiyar community celebrated me as the awardee. I was really ecstatic. I am eternally grateful for the love and support of Aruntatiyar, the original inhabitants of Tamil Nadu. Many thanks to *Dinamani* (Delhi Edition) daily, Aruntatiyar media and all other media for spreading the news of the award.

Readers of this book may feel the need for a chronological history of Aruntatiyar. Prof Basil Xavier, who contributed to this book, also identified and pointed out this gap. This legitimate deficiency will surely be rectified in the next edition of this book. I humbly record that there is room for alternative thinking and research from new angles in this book on the subject of Tamil Nadu Aruntatiyar history.

I welcome reader's healthy feedback, criticism and comments on this book. They will help me in improving the quality of the book and bring out the next edition.

Thanks.

New Delhi - 110021
June, 2023

With warm regards
Prof S. Seenivasan
Email: drseenivasan@gmail.com

Translator's Note

It is indeed a great pleasure in translating a text from Tamil to English. It is doubly gratifying to translate a historical text based on ethnographic study from Tamil to English. Having said this, the story of Oṇṭivīraṉ, a Dalit hero whose historical facts of life and death have not yet been popular not just in India but also in his home state - Tamil Nadu. Most of us know about Vīrapāṇṭiya Kaṭṭapom'maṉ, Tīraṉ Ciṉṉamalai, Marutu Brothers, Vāñcinātaṉ, Marutanāyakam [with the recent cinematic hype, we also seem to know more about Marutanāyakam alias Khan Sahib]. But unsung Dalit champions such as Kuyili, Oṇṭivīraṉ, Cērvāraṉ, and many others who were equally or more valorous, brave, swashbuckling than these known ones are still not brought to light. In short, the history of a large number of unknown warriors, conquerors, champions is still unknown. In this backdrop, Prof Seenivasan's valiant effort to put the spotlight on some of the most exciting and chivalrous Aruntatiyar commanders namely Oṇṭivīraṉ, Kuyili, Muttuvīraṉ, and others, deserves appreciation.

This book dwells upon another interesting aspect apart from just introducing some of the unsung heroes who fought for India's freedom movement. This is the first such attempt, in my knowledge, to inform the readers that such heroes' life and their history were overlooked just because of their caste background. By exposing this very fact which is a communal side of the story, the author unpacks the majoritarian tyrannical discourse which resulted from the pride and prejudices of the caste-ridden society in India in general and in Tamil Nadu in particular. Thus, he exposes the mindset of the mainstream historians and their lackadaisical approach as far as subaltern history is concerned. It is necessary to mention here that Dalit stories present not just a different view of the reality, but also function to outrage the custodians of class and caste. It is important to understand in this context that the very act of writing may be considered a means of resistance against oppressive structures.

Another interesting aspect of this book is that the author had written in a jargon-free, easy-to-read style that is accessible to a general readership. This necessarily also meant that explicit articulation of theoretical arguments be largely kept out, and the narrative should unfold as a story, in a chronological scheme. But Prof Seenivasan has intelligently balanced and thus juxtaposed both theory and history. Kudos to Prof S. Seenivasan for intertwining these two elements of a book.

It is noteworthy to mention some interesting and important aspects of this book : (a) that the source book *Tamiḻaka Aruntatiyar: Varalāṟum Vāḻvum* has been declared as the *Best Book of 2021* by the Government of Tamil Nadu, (b) that the author has been conferred *Periyar Award (2020)* by Āti Tamiḻar Party, Chennai, for his contribution towards the development of marginal sections of the society of Tamil Nadu, (c) that the author has received the prestigious *Dr B.R. Ambedkar Excellency Service National Award 2022* by Bharatiya Dalit Sahitya Academy (BDSA) in recognition of the commendable literary, social and cultural services rendered by him for the upliftment of downtrodden, oppressed and depressed people of the country and (d) that the author (Prof S. Seenivasan) of the above-mentioned book has been awarded as the *Best Author of 2021* by the Government of Tamil Nadu.

Having grown up in a Tamil-speaking household, when I first read Dr Seenivasan's *Tamiḻaka Aruntatiyar: Varalāṟum Vāḻvum (*An Ethnographic Study of Aruntatiyars of Tamil Nadu), I could certainly almost hear echoes of colloquial Tamil which is called Koṭuntamiḻ. In spite of being a Koṭuntamiḻ speaker I had more difficulty in translating such registers of colloquial Tamil than the Centamiḻ [standard (ised) Tamil]. In fact, I have given up translating three cited Dalit folk ballads. Why? Because they were not just colloquial but were sung in eighteenth century Tamil. Meanings for some of the words and expressions are not found in any of the online dictionaries. The real challenge posed by the author was not at the level of semantics but it was also at the level of hermeneutics. Though I have understood the global meaning of all the Dalit folk songs, tales and ballads, it was still not possible for me to explain them, in the first place, to myself and then to the prospective readers in/of English. I did realise that 'translation is the most intimate act of reading and one has to surrender to the text[1]' while translating this particular text. But the surrendering aspect of the 'whole process' is quite problematic. As a translator, who is also a free thinker like any writer, is involved deeply in finding the best suitable equivalence to the text in the target language and hence, my approach being target oriented translation and hermeneutical in nature, I don't think I would have to necessarily surrender to the source text. Overcoming the hermeneutical problems in the act of translation was a real test. I leave it to the readers, translation experts and traductologists to decide whether I have passed the test.

For kind attention of the readers who know Tamil and English. The title of the source text *Tamiḻaka Aruntatiyar : Varalāṟum vāḻvum* has been interpreted and not translated directly from Tamil. This decision has been taken in consultation with the author of this book. In fact, we (translator and author) both discussed at length the most important aspect of translation what is called translation ethics: Should a title of the original work be translated with utmost fidelity or can it be done with the interpretative theory of translation? Why did we raise this question? Because the object of translation is the sense born out of the merging of language actualised in a text and the receptor's relevant knowledge. The outcome of the discussion brought five different versions as far as the translation of the title is concerned. We zeroed in on the one which appears in the translated text. Needless to say, the

1. https://biblioteka.filg.uj.edu.pl/documents/2205554/33980917/SPIVAK%2C%20 GAYATRI%20CHAKRAVORTY.pdf

translation of the whole text was carried out the way we have deliberated and reviewed the title. Another major modification that was done in the translated version of the book is the change in the chapterisation. Tamil text had six chapters whereas the translation has eight chapters. After a detailed discussion and debate, the author and the translator have decided to make some changes and increase it to eight chapters. I hope that readers (those who have read the source text) will appreciate these changes and benefit from the work we (author and translator) have done.

Prof Ajith Kanna
JNU, New Delhi
May, 2023
Email: ajitsulo@yahoo.com

Chapter - 1

Ethnography: History and Definition

Anthropology is the study of human body, language, culture and archaeological record. In short, anthropology is a complete science that studies the human being. This scientific research called 'Anthropology' has begun in the countries of the world in the early part of the nineteenth century.

American anthropologists have defined this into two major divisions as cultural anthropology and social anthropology. Ethnography forms one of the significant components of cultural anthropology. The term 'Iṉavaraiviyal' is used in Tamil as equivalent to the English term 'ethnography'. Ethnography is based on the culture of people living in Grecophone countries. The Greek scholar Herodotus (484 - 425 BC) is considered to be the father of Greek ethnography. He traveled to different countries of the world and is known as the father of Greek history.

The term 'Iṉavaraiviyal' in Tamil is derived from English through Greek. The English word Ethnography is derived from the Greek words 'ethnos', 'graphein' and 'Ethnos' means 'race', 'ethnic group', 'people'. Anthropologist Paktavatcala Pārati also defines 'Graphein' as 'writing' or 'drawing'.

Definitions of Ethnography

The following can be listed as ethnographic definitions put forward by scholars:

1. American anthropologists define ethnography as the complete study of culture about a group or community living with shared biological resources.
2. Ethnographic study deals with the distribution, origin, migration, ethnic identity elements, psychological elements, social divisions, lifestyle, occupation etc. of a particular race or community.
3. Ethnography is a complete compilation of the culture, lifestyle, beliefs, knowledge, customs etc. of a particular community. The ethnographic data thus compiled will be descriptive in nature.
4. Ethnography is a form of writing that is based on field studies and describes the characteristics of human social phenomena. Ethnography is the study of a particular ethnic group or people.
5. Ethnography is also the study of a particular society or culture through fieldwork. Books were published on this basis during the colonial rule.
6. It was the French anthropologist Louis Dumont's attempt to make ethnography open and dense.
7. Malinowski, a Polish anthropologist who studied the Trobrianders living in the islands of the Western Pacific, used their family nature, anatomical ignorance, kinship meaning, important economic rituals, etc. as basic elements to understand the ethnography of the people.
8. Ethnography is a written picture of a society, a creation of truth about a society. Ethnography is to bring out and realise the cultures that are frozen in the minds of the people.

Elements of Ethnography

1. Photo/Film
2. Encyclopedia

3. Processual
4. Dialectics
5. Holistic
6. Day-to-day activities and other cycles
7. Particularistic
8. Historical
9. Examining the system of rules.

Ethnography in the Indian Context - An Overview

Anthropology also appeared as a side effect of the establishment of colonialism in India. The British, whose main objective was to subjugate India, exploit the Indian economy, monopolise trade, increase revenue and spread religion, did not focus on regulating Indian society. Following the first revolt against British imperialism in India (10.05.1857) the British government began collecting data on all the communities under its rule. Histories of various parts of India were written and codified in the English language by the English authorities. These were published as manuals, handbooks or gazetteers. The aim of the British government was to regulate the Indian society and keep it under control.

The British tried to gather local information about the Indian people in their visionary plan to continue to dominate India. As an immediate result, Indian people were classified and their race, language, caste, religion, customs, kinship, ritual etc. were recorded. Subsequently, in the 1880s, separate manuals were prepared for all the districts of the Madras province. The first census was taken in 1871 as an extension of the plan to regulate Indian society. Caste and religion were the basic units of the Indian population in the census data collected by the British. These efforts of the British were processed in all sections of the British administration.

"Colin Mackenzie, a colonial official, began compiling

information on the tribal population of Tamil Nadu as part of the process of declassifying Indian society. These include 3000 copperplates engraved with official information about land granted by a king or a historically significant message such as a king's victory, 1568 manuscripts in 15 languages, 8076 inscriptions, 2630 paintings, 78 maps, 6218 coins and 102 statues. Out of these 1534 traces are about Tamil Nadu", says Bakthavatchala Bharathi (2004:7-8). Bakthavatchala Bharathi mentions that there are 16 traces about the tribes of Tamil Nadu in the government's archive of downstream traces.

In 1885, the British Government of India issued an order requiring Indian states to carry out ethnographic surveys of their respective states. According to the policy decision of the British Government, the then Curator of the Madras Museum Thurston, Edgar (1855 - 1935) started compiling ethnographic data for South India from 1901 onwards. He compiled various types of information such as social structure, anatomy, marriages, rituals, religious beliefs, panchayat-justice-punishment systems and customs of the people spread across various levels from the Khonds in the North to the Southern part of Kaṉṉiyākumari. Thurston (1907) published a part of the details thus compiled in two volumes under the title *Ethnographic Notes in Southern India*. Later, in 1909, he wrote and published seven volumes titled *Caste and Tribes of Southern India*.

Thus, Thurston described the colonial state as 'The Ethnographic State' because of the massive collection and classification of anthropological reports (Bakthavatchala Bharathi, 2002: XXIX). It should be noted here that the British directly used ethnography in the administration of India. Kathryn Kaif refers to anthropology, which includes ethnography, as the 'child of imperialism', states A. Sivasubramanian. (1995:3).

Ethnography in the context of Tamil Nadu - An Overview

A number of ethnographic studies have been carried out in post-colonial South India, particularly in Tamil Nadu. Most of them were written by westerners. Among them: *Study of Agrarian Society of Kongu Region* - Brenda E. F. Beck, *Study of Maravar* - Anthony Good, *Study of Madurai Meenakshiyaman* - Chris Fuller, *Study of Urbanisation* - Rudner David, *Study of Nadars* - Dennis Roy Templeman, *Study of Working-class People* - Michael Moffat and Robert Deliège, *Study of Regional Castes of Trichy* - Karin Kapadia, *Study of Social Structure* - Cathelin Co. etc. are subtle ethnographic studies on Tamils.

Kondaiyamkottai Maravar: A Dravidian Tribe of Tinnevelly, South India (1903) - Fawcett, *An Untouchable Community in South India: Structure and Consensus* (1979) - Michelle Moffatt, *A South Indian Subcaste : Social organisation and religion of the Piramalai Kallar* (1986) - Dumont, Louis, *Bonds Lost : Subordination, Conflict and Mobilisation in Rural South India from 1900 to 1970* (1997) - Gunnel Katerlof are some of the studies that were carried out with anthropological theoretical nuances.

Following the Westerners, Indians themselves attempted to write Indian ethnography. Bakthavatchala Bharathi alleges that the ethnographic studies written in such a way lack a descriptive approach without a theoretical technique and therefore the ethnographic method with a theoretical understanding and analytical focus has not been widespread. This was considered the greatest weakness and setback for the field of ethnography. *The slaves of the soil in southern India* (1893) - T.B. Paṇdiyaṉ, *A Study on Naarkudi Vellalar* (1920) - T. Aṟumuga Nayaṉar Piḷḷai's *A Study of Narikkuravar* (1978) - and research works of K. Srinivasa Sharma, etc. were pioneering ethnographic works in Tamil. With the advent of socio-cultural studies and anthropological studies in Tamil Nadu folk literature significant ethnographic studies were also carried out. Among them: Marc's *Aruntatiyar Vāḻum Varalāṟu* (2001), Karasoor Padmabarathi's *Narikkuṟavar Iṉavaraiviyal* (2004), Aru. Paramasivam's *Paruvata Rājakula Mīṉavariṉ Aṟiyappaṭāta Marapukaḷum Kāṇikaḷum* (2003), *Paravatar Iṉa Mīṭṭuruvākka Varaiviyal* (2005), *Teṉṉintiya Iṉa Oppumaiyiyal*,

(2004). B. Rajeṣh's *Yātavar Iṉavaviraiviyal* (2004), M. Gnaṉathai's *Maṟavar Kataippāṭalkaḷ: Iṉavaraiviyal Āyvu* (2006), A. Dhaṉanjeyan's *Viḷimpunilai Vaḻakkāṟukaḷ: Iṉavaraiviyal Āyvu* (2006), P. Govindasamy's *Liṅkāyattukaḷ: Iṉavaraiviyal Āyvu* (2006), A. Randhir Kumar's *Nellai Nakara Aruntatiyar Kuṟitta Iṉavaraiviyal Āyvu* (2008), V. Paṉṉeerselvam's *Aruntatiyarkaḷ Yār? : Ōr Varalāṟṟu Pārvai* (2008), Father Masilamaṇi Adigaḷ's *Vempakkōṭṭai Aruntatiyarkaḷiṉ Vāḻviyal : Iṉavaraiviyal Āyvu* (2008), N. Murugesapaṇdiyaṉ's *Kuṭukuṭuppaikkārar Iṉavaraiviyal* (2009), Maṇi K. Paṉṉeerselvam's *Kuṟavar Paḻaṅkuṭi : Iṉavaraiviyal Āyvu* (2009), Kalaiselvi's *Caṅka Ilakkiyattil Maṟavarkaḷ* (2011), Bakthavatchala Bharathi's *Pāṇar Iṉavaraiviyal* (2012), K. Ragupathy's *Āti Maruttuvar Cavara Toḻilāḷarākkappaṭṭa Varalāṟu* (2012), V.R. Pavithra's *Pulaiyar Iṉavaraiviyal* (2013), Ṣōpaṉā's *Paṉaicār Ulakam: Nāṭār Iṉavaraiviyal* (2013), M.A. Krishnamurthy's *Aruntatiyar Camūkattiṉ aṟiya Varalāṟu* (2014), T. Rejit Kumar's *Maruttuvar Varalāṟum Vaḻakkāṟukaḷum* (2014), A. Sivasubramaniyaṉ's *Tamiḻ Vaṇṇār: Varalāṟum Vaḻakkāṟukaḷum* (2014), T. Dhaṉanjeyaṉ's *Tamiḻakattil Purata Vaṇṇārkaḷ* (2015), A. Revathy's *Koṅkunāṭṭu Tamiḻ Vaṇṇār Iṉavaraiviyal (Īrōṭu Māvaṭṭam)* (2016), C. Lakṣmanaṉ and K. Ragupathy's *Tīṇṭāmaikkuḷ Tīṇṭāmai: Putirai Vaṇṇār Vāḻvum Iruppum* (2016), A. Krishnamurthy's *Arunthathiyar: The Great Leather workers of Tamil Nadu - Life & History* (2017), N. Deepa Raṇi's *Tamiḻ Tolkuṭi Varalāṟu: Iruḷar (Toṇṭai Maṇṭalam)* (2017), C. Karuṇakaraṉ's *Āyar Vāḻviyal* (2017), M. Robert's *Iṉavaraiviyal Nōkkil Narikkuṟavarkaḷiṉ Vāḻviyal* (2018), S. Basil Xavier's *Ethnophilosophising in India: A Study on Aruntatiyars* (2020) are notable ethnographic studies.

Tamil Department at Bharathiar University, Tamil Nadu organised a lecture series on '*Literature and Ethnography*' in 2019. A collection of papers read in this conference is soon to be published.

Use of Ethnographic Research

Anthropologist Bakthavatchala Bharathi surmises that ethnographic research can be useful for measuring the changes in society and for the understanding of social change that needs to be planned in the future.

- Ethnographic study of a particular community can reveal a community's history and culture. In this way, there will be a chance for other ethnic groups to know the unwritten, hidden and neglected history and culture of that particular ethnic group. Ethnographic studies help to eliminate caste-based stratification and achieve equality.
- Ethnography plays an important role in the study of the society, culture and customs of the people living in the plains, forests, mountains and islands. Ethnography is also a treasury that provides data needed for the fields of knowledge such as social anthropology, cultural anthropology, and national jurisprudence.
- In order to gather data and observe the life of a particular community, it is necessary for the ethnographer to have a close relationship with the community and to know the language they speak. The strength of his relationship with the mothers will determine the success of data collection. When the data collected in such a way becomes an ethnographic book, 'people of other races and castes can clearly know many subtle messages about a particular race or caste', says A. Sivasubramaniyan (1995:3).
- Ethnographic information can be used to understand one ethnic group about another group. Through this, there is a chance to avoid the daily caste conflicts in the country and bring peace. Such ethnographic studies can contribute to the cultural development and historical recovery of the marginalised, particularly Dalit, oppressed and disadvantaged peoples.

- When the younger generation understands about other people apart from his race, the attitude of respecting human beings as human beings will prevail and brotherhood will prevail among fellow human beings. It requires the recovery and dissemination of oppressed, marginalised and Dalit social histories.
- By recovering and rediscovering the true history and culture of the people through ethnographic studies, it can make a great contribution to the field of Tamil studies and knowledge.

Ethnography and Ballads

It is the need of today's times that folklore studies has developed as a field that studies all folk traditions including folk ballads on a scientific basis. Ballads, one of the folk traditions, originated in the sixteenth century AD and has continued to grow till date. Ballads with characteristics such as plot, character background, etc., is interesting and dramatised.

These stories depict the history and lifestyle of various tribes, their work and sacrifices. Along with them, the life, culture, society, caste system etc. of the respective country people are also highlighted. The social contradictions prevailing at the time of the birth of ballads and the inequalities of life are the foundations for the birth of ballads. Narratives are based on events that occur in society. These are the sources of various contradictions in the society. These explain how such contradictions can be resolved. Various studies have been carried out on narratives, but no ethnographic study has been conducted to study the narratives. Some of the Tamil stories can be studied under a separate category called 'Dalit Ballads'.

In every district of Tamil Nadu, ballads through songs have appeared according to the political, social and economic conditions of the respective times. The heroes of this story are unique in every way. Ethnographic study deals with the distribution, origin, migration, ethnic identity, psychological elements, social divisions, lifestyle, occupation, etc. of a particular race or community.

History – Obscuration of identity

The purpose of ethnography is to categorise the culture of one particular ethnic group to be understood by another ethnic group. Speaking caste is one thing, ethnography of caste is another. History that has already been written is mostly the history of kings and dominant caste leaders. Much of the history in written form today is written by the upper class/caste Hindus and is written with a view. Even in written history, the history and life of Dalits, has not been documented. Downtrodden people have a long history. It is deliberately hidden from being recorded, blacked out. This shows that the history of the people of Tamil Nadu was not recorded unbiasedly.

Historian S. Manickam in his historical book *Conspiracy of Silence: Historical Black-out of the Dalits of India with particular Reference to Tamil Nadu* has pointed out that the way of life of the Dalits has been blacked out in the history of the ruling class. It is worth recalling at this point that their history has been distorted and explained without evidence (I. Muthaiah, 2008:85). African and its peoples' histories were covered up by white imperialism saying, "You have no philosophical legacy and there is nothing in writing to support your history". It is worth noting here that imperialism, which prevented African history from being recorded and African people from communicating, anticipated the written history of African people.

Hence, the situation has arisen to re-examine the already written history. As the subaltern community became literate and aware of their living conditions, they began to criticise the violent expressions of the ruling class, historiography and history. Realising that their history and identities have been obscured (sort of deconstructing) in such histories. I. Muthaiah's work is worth considering here.

Restoration of folk narratives

In today's environment, historians are reiterating the fact that history should be written as 'History From Below'. Finding the history of oppressed communities from written histories is biased. Also, V. Paṉṉeerselvam (2008:1) thinks that the history of the people can be the true history of the people, and the history of the kings was taught apart from it, and there is also the opinion that it is wrong.

Folk narratives help us to know the antiquity of a race. The reconstruction of the history of the people of the base with the help of national advocates can be legitimate and authentic. Basic data for writing history of Dalit people should be sought and identified from Dalit people themselves. The oral traditions found among the Dalits are a good source for this. Narratives about Dalits are of great help in writing the history of Dalits.

The social history of the Dalit people will be revealed when the Dalit literature, especially the Dalit ballads, is analyzed within the grammatical framework of 'ethnography'. Ethnographic study reveals the fact that Dalits have an ethnic history similar to that of the dominant castes.

Through these, the social history and cultural roots of the Dalit people can be fully explored. It can be seen that the history of the oppressed castes is being constructed as an alternative to the history of the dominant castes by adopting the existing social, economic and political systems using oral sources such as ballads. The history of castes like Nāṭār, Tēvēntirakula Veḷḷāḷar, Paṟaiyar, Aruntatiyar, Vēṭuva Kavuṇṭar, etc. have been written down with oral forms such as ballads as evidences. Such an alternative history has the historical characteristics of the dominant caste. That is, in the past, being members of the royal dynasty, having all the honours and rights of the dominant caste, being landlords, etc., have been compiled from oral forms such as ballads and written as an alternative history (I. Muthaiah, 2008:100).

Dalit Ethnographic Ballads: An Introduction

Countless ballads are found all over Tamil Nadu. Ballads have appeared in each district according to the political, social and economic conditions of the respective times. The heroes and characters of these stories are unique in every way. There are many social ballads in Tamil Nadu and there are more than twenty ballads in oral and written form. These oral and written ballads are popular among the caste groups of Kavuṇṭar, Kaḷḷar, Kōṉār, Nāṭār, Maṟavar, Veḷḷāḷar, Paḷḷar, Kam'mā Nāyakkar, Paratavar, Mutaliyār, Kuṟavar, Cakkiliyar, Akamuṭaiyār, Brahmin, Uṭaiyār, Vaṇṇār, Kampaḷattu Nāyakkar, etc. The following sources can be cited as a proof:

1. Maturaivīraṉ Katai - Aruntatiyar X Maṉṉar (Madurai District) [Maturaivīraṉ's Story - Aruntatiyar X Maṉṉar (Madurai District)]
2. Muttuppaṭṭaṉ Katai - Aruntatiyar X Pirāmaṇar (Tirunelveli District) [Muttuppaṭṭaṉ's Story - Aruntatiyar X Pirāmaṇar (Tirunelveli District)]
3. Ciṉṉattampi Katai - Aruntatiyar X Veḷḷāḷar (Tirunelveli District) [Ciṉṉattampi's Story - Aruntatiyar X Veḷḷāḷar (Tirunelveli District)]
4. Kautala Māṭaṉ Katai - Aruntatiyar X Tēvar (Kaṉṉiyakumari District) [Kautala Māṭaṉ's Story - Aruntatiyar X Tēvar (Kaṉṉiyakumari District)]
5. Kāttavarāyaṉ Katai - Paṟaiyar X Pirāmaṇar (Trichy District) [Kāttavarāyaṉ's Story - Paṟaiyar X Pirāmaṇar (Trichy District)]
6. Maikēl Am'māḷ Katai - Paḷḷar X Uṭaiyār (Ramanathapuram District) [Maikēl Ammāḷ's Story - Paḷḷar X Uṭaiyār (Ramanathapuram District)]
7. Taṭivīra Cuvāmi Kataippāṭalkaḷ [Taṭivīra Cuvāmi Folk Ballads]

8. Ciṉṉaṇaiñcāṉ Kataippāṭal - Vaṇṇār X Aracar Kuḷam [Ciṉṉaṇaiñcāṉ Folk Ballads - Vaṇṇār X Aracar Kuḷam]
9. Vaṇṇāra Kolai Cintu - Vaṇṇār X Kauṇṭar (Selam District)
10. Meccum Perumāḷ Pāṇṭiyaṉ Kataippāṭal - Vaṇṇār X Maṟavar (Tirunelveli District) [Meccum Perumāḷ Pāṇṭiyaṉ's Folk Ballads - Vaṇṇār X Maṟavar (Tirunelveli District)]

All these works are available in print.

Unknown Aruntatiyar Folk Ballads

It is traditional to call a ballad written about a particular race as a 'regional ballad'. Hence, it is appropriate to call these 'ethnographic narratives'. It is possible to find many unpublished ballads about the Aruntatiyars, a major section of the Dalit community, in various districts of Tamil Nadu. However, below are the ballads about Aruntatiyar community collected from southern districts Madurai, Sivagangai, Tirunelveli, Thuthukkudi, Kanniyakumari of Tamil Nadu.

1. Oṇṭivīraṉ Kataippāṭal - Aruntatiyar X Maṟavar (Tirunelveli District) [Oṇṭivīraṉ's Folk Ballads - Aruntatiyar X Maṟavar (Tirunelveli District)]
2. Kautala Māṭaṉ Kataippāṭal - Aruntatiyar X Tēvar (Kaṉṉiyākumāri District) [Kautala Māṭaṉ's Folk Ballads - Aruntatiyar X Tēvar (Kaṉṉiyakumari District)]
3. Cērvāraṉcāmi Kataippāṭal - Aruntatiyar X Vēḷāḷar (Tirunelveli District) [Cērvāraṉcāmi's Folk Ballads - Aruntatiyar X Vēḷāḷar (Tirunelveli District)]
4. Māyakkaruvi Cāmāyi Ammaṉ's Folk Ballads (Sivagangai District) [Māyakkaruvi cāmāyi am'maṉ kataippāṭal (Sivagangai District)]
5. Rāmapakaṭai - Ciṉṉattampi Kataippāṭal (Tirunelveli District) [Rāmapakaṭai - Ciṉṉattampi Folk Ballads (Tirunelveli District)]

6. Ciṉṉakuruvaṉ - Periyakuruvaṉ Kataippāṭal (Tūttukkuṭi District) [Ciṉṉakuruvaṉ - Periyakuruvaṉ Folk Ballads (Thutukkudi District)]

The story of Maturaivīraṉ reveals the social dilemma of the Catriyars and Cakkiliyars, the story of Muttuppāṭṭaṉ reveals the social dilemma of the Brahmins and Cakkiliyars. The story of Ciṉṉattampi which shows the social problem of Veḷḷāḷars and Cakkiliyars, and the story of Cērvāraṉ, the story of Kautala Māṭaṉ which shows the social problem of Maṟavars and Cakkiliyars, and the story of Oṇṭivīraṉ, the story of Kāttavarāyaṉ which depicts the social problem of Brahmins and Paṟaiyars, and the story of Michael Am'māḷ which depicts the social corruption of Uṭaiyārs and Paḷḷars are known. All these ballads reveal the work done by the Dalit people of Tamil Nadu for the country and society, their lifestyles, customs, cultural elements, characteristics, etc.

Chapter - 2

Aruntatiyars: First Inhabitants of Tamil Nadu

Socio-anthropological, ethnohistorical, ethnographic and epigraphic studies of every caste in the world is one of the most urgent needs of today's times. It is only through such efforts that 'Dalitism' can grow and evolve into a history of struggle. Studies like these could be the seeds for Dalitism to emerge. History that has already been written is mostly the history of kings and dominant caste leaders. Most of the written histories now in written form are written with a more elitist perspective. Indeed, history is not made by kings or rulers; on the contrary, real history emerges from the history from below.

Nature of Written History

In general, the writers of Tamil Nadu history have focused more on telling the history of the royal families. The views of Subramanian who wrote about the Sangam period, N. Rajamanickanar who wrote about the Pallavā period, K.A. Sadasivapandarathar who wrote about the Cōḻā period and historians such as Neelakanda Sasthiri have narrated the history of Tamil Nadu as the history of royal families. Such views are also found in the books of T.V. Mahalingam and S. Krishnaswamy who wrote about the Vijayanagara Empire and Nāyakkar kings. A. Ramaswamy says that the histories written using the inscriptions that recorded the messages about the wealth, gifts, donations, rights and punishments given by the kings, and the copperplates that reveal the lineages of the kings, can only be written in that manner. In the history of Tamil Nadu, the true history of Tamil Nadu is the history of the people belonging to the lower rung of the Tamil society and not the just the history of the kings and rulers.

History from Below

In today's era, history has to start from the grassroots. Even in the written history of Dalits, Tamil Nadu's Aruntatiyar history has not been discussed much. But the Aruntatiyar people have had a glorious past and a long history of their own. An environment has arisen to restore it. The history of oppressed communities from written histories is biased. Instead, the reconstruction of Dalit history with the help of inscriptions can be legitimate and authentic. In that way, the history of Tamil Nadu's original inhabitants, the Aruntatiyars, who have been neglected in history, can be constructed through the oral history of the people, inscriptions, folk arts such as folk narratives, and ballads. Through these elements, the social history and cultural roots of the Aruntatiyars can be fully explored.

Tamil Nadu is inhabited by people who speak many languages. Apart from the natives of Tamil Nadu, people who have migrated from other states of India have been living in Tamil Nadu for many generations. They speak their mother tongues Malayalam, Telugu, Kannada, Saurashtra and Hindi along with Tamil. Castes such as Reṭṭiyār, Nāyakkar, Nāyuṭu, Ceṭṭiyār, Cakkiliyar, Pōyar, Oṭar, Visvakarmā, Uṟumikkārar, etc. who are said to have migrated to Tamil Nadu from other states speak Telugu. These people, who have been living in Tamil Nadu for many generations have learned to speak Telugu, read and write along with speaking Tamil. But there are great differences between the Telugu dialects spoken by them. There are differences not only at the regional level but even village wise. The immigrants living in Tamil Nadu are not keen in learning to read and write their mother tongue. They speak their mother tongue at home and Tamil outside.

According to the Anthropological Survey of India, there are 4635 communities in post-colonial India today. According to the ethnographic study 'People of India' published by the Anthropological Review of India, there are 364 communities in Tamil Nadu. The Government of Tamil Nadu has prepared a list of castes living in Tamil Nadu as Tribals, Scheduled Castes, Backward Classes and Most Backward Castes for reservation in education and employment opportunities. (Primary Census Abstract - 1995). Among the castes included in this list, 78 castes are classified as low castes. Government registers refer to these as Scheduled Castes. Among these, three castes, namely Paḷḷars, Paṟaiyars and Cakkiliyars are more in number than other lower castes.

History of Tamil Nadu's Aruntatiyars

Among the three castes in Tamil Nadu, namely Paḷḷar, Paṟaiyar and Cakkiliyar, the most prominent is the 'Cakkiliyar' caste. This caste group is also known as Aruntatiyar. These castes, who speak Tamil and Telugu, live widely in the western districts of Tamil Nadu and to a lesser extent in the southern districts of Tamil Nadu. In Tamil Nadu, the Aruntatiyars, known as Cakkiliyars, are still living in the lower ranks of the untouchable castes. "They have been kept in a low position to the extent of slave labour for the Paḷḷars in the Southern Tamil Nadu districts and the Paṟaiyars in the Northern Tamil Nadu districts. The people of Aruntatiyar, who are fastidious, loyal, trustworthy and fearful, are pushed to the point of thinking that slavery is the right thing and are very backward in education and living without improving their economic status. These people of Aruntatiyar community are faceless and faceless even in history", says M.A. Kriṣhnamurthy (2014:135-142).

Documents related to the Aruntatiyars

Almost a hundred years ago, in the 1920s, the name 'Cakkiliyar' was considered as a derogatory term in society. Roa Sahib L.C. Gurusami, a Cakkiliyar community pioneer, proposed to the then government to change that stigma. In 1922, when the

Justice Party was in power in Tamil Nadu, a decree was issued to change the names of some castes based on a resolution passed in the combined Madras Provincial Assembly. At that time, the people who were involved in the leather industry, who were known as Cem'māṉ, Cakkili, Pakaṭai, Mātāri and Mātikā, were renamed as 'Aruntatiyar' by the government. (Law (General), Department G.O. Ms.No.817, Dated: 25.03.1922). This name is also registered in the Government document (Gazette). After nearly ninety years, the Tamil Nadu government has issued an order to merge the castes of Aruntatiyar, Cakkiliyar, Mātāri, Mātik, Pakaṭai, Tōṭṭi and Āti Āntirā and renamed them as 'Aruntatiyar'. (G.O.Ms.No.55. Personnel and Administrative Reforms, 8th April, 2010). However, the old caste names persist today in government documents and practice without disappearing from the case.

The Aruntatiyars comprising the above seven caste groups living in Tamil Nadu can be divided into three groups as Telugu-speaking Aruntatiyars, Kannada-speaking Aruntatiyars and Tamil-speaking Aruntatiyars based on their place of residence and language. They are not literate in Telugu and Kannada languages. On the contrary, they are native speakers of Tamil.

A dig into the past and a journey forward

Ethnographic study reveals the fact that the Aruntatiyars have an ethnic history similar to that of the dominant castes. In Tamil Nadu, Paḷḷar, (Tēvēntirakula Veḷḷāḷar), Paṟaiyar (Āti Tirāviṭar) and Cakkiliyar (Aruntatiyar) are known as the lower castes of Tamil Nadu. Native Aruntatiyar history, stories, folk ballads, literature, celebrations etc. are available for this community. Through these we can trace the heritage and roots of these people. The Aruntatiyars were not inferior in the beginning, but in course of time were brought down by the dominant castes. The traditional occupation of the Aruntatiyars was not scavenging but they lived as peasants, zamindars, army commanders, warriors and respectable servants at kings's courts and palaces. This chapter constructs the ethnic history of the Cakkilyars, the original inhabitants of Tamil Nadu.

Aruntatiyars of Tamil Nadu: Origins and Diaspora

Apart from great rulers such as Cēraṉ, Cōḻaṉ and Pāṇṭiyaṉ, many local chieftains also ruled in Tamil Nadu. Among them there are also the Vēḷir sects. Among these Vēḷir sects there is also a sect called 'Ātiyar'. They ruled Takaṭūr region. The region was called 'Vaṭuku Nāṭu'. The Aruntatiyars are the descendants of this Ātiyar sect. The name Ātiyar is the name given to Aruntatiyar. The king of Ātiyar clan was called Mā + Ātiyar = Mātiyar. Mātiyar is another name given to Aruntatiyar.

Atiyamāṉ was the greatest king of the Mātiyar clan. The Aruntatiyars, also known as First Inhabitants of Tamil country, came from the 'Ātiyar clan' of King Atiyamāṉ. The question arises, why do they speak Telugu and Kannada if the Aruntatiyars are First Inhabitants of Tamil country? In Karnataka, Kannada dialects are mostly mixed with Tamil and Telugu. For that reason Kannadigas cannot be considered Tamils or Telugus. Takaṭūr, where the ancestors of the Aruntatiyars lived, is situated in Tarmapuri region of present Tamil Nadu. It is also known as "Vaṭuku Nāṭu". When the southern part of the country was a united region, this Vaṭuku Nāṭu was shared borders with Andhra region and with Karnataka. When Vaṭuku Nāṭu was divided into separate regions, one part joined Tamil Nadu, another part joined Andhra, and another part joined Karnataka.

Although Dharmapuri was a short distance away from the road to Karnataka, the Aruntatiyars did not go there much. Fewer people migrated within Karnataka. A large number of Aruntatiyars migrated to Andhra border areas, which are more mountainous and water-rich than Dharmapuri, in search of work for survival. A few others migrated for business. They have stayed and lived in the places they visited in those days when there was no transportation facility. *Paṭṭiṉappālai, Naṟṟiṇai*, and *Cilappatikāram* refer to the people who move from one country to another for reasons such as war, natural disasters, survival, work, and business as 'diasporic community'.

The Aruntatiyars who migrated there did not go to the central region of Andhra and Karnataka and stayed in Andhra - Karnataka - Tamil Nadu border areas. The Aruntatiyars who migrated from Andhra Pradesh and Karnataka had to learn their mother tongue Telugu and Kannada for their daily needs. They went to school at Andhra border and did not learn Kannada and Telugu properly. Instead they only learned the spoken language there. Kannada and Telugu Aruntatiyar do not know where quality copper is made. Till now, the Aruntatiyars have been speaking Tamil, a mixture of Kannada and Telugu. All of us should understand that none of the Aruntatiyars living in Tamil Nadu know Kannada and Telugu script. This can be seen from the fact that there is a huge difference between the colloquial words used by the people of Andhra Pradesh and the colloquial words used by the Aruntatiyars of Tamil Nadu. Migrant Tamil Aruntatiyars, in the course of time, came to Tamil Nadu in many periods due to the increase in rainfall and prosperity in Tamil Nadu and due to various circumstances. These are the people who live today in Tamil Nadu as Kannada-speaking Aruntatiyars and Telugu-speaking Aruntatiyars. That is why the Telugu and Kannada spoken by the Aruntatiyars are borderline Kannada and Telugu dialects. It is worth noting here that the Telugu language spoken by the people in the inner districts of the united Andhra Pradesh varies regionally.

The Aruntatiyar people of Tamil Nadu are well versed in Telugu and Kannada colloquial languages. It is noteworthy here to say that the Aruntatiyar who live in the northern and western districts of Tamil Nadu speak a mixture of Tamil, Telugu and Kannada, and the Aruntatiyar who live in the southern districts speak a completely mixed language of Tamil and Telugu without Kannada. Kannada and Telugu speaking communities live in large numbers in Tamil Nadu. These people speak Kannada and Telugu but are not literate.

Thus, calling the Aruntatiyar Tamil residents who came back to Andhra in search of livelihood and speak Tamil with a Telugu tone and sound as Telugu and labelling them as migrants is nothing but an attempt to alienate the Aruntatiyars who are original Tamils. Aruntatiyars are the original inhabitants of Tamil Nadu, the original Tamils are the history of Tamil country. The fact that none of the ancestors of the Aruntatiyars knew how to read and write Telugu is a clear proof that they are not Telugus but descendants of the Tamil country. Eminent scholar P. Kōvintaṉār defines Tamils as people who are born and speak Tamil as their mother tongue. According to P. Govindanar's definition, all the Aruntatiyars currently living in Tamil Nadu are considered to be Tamils. Just because the Aruntatiyars speak Telugu, it cannot be assumed that they are not Tamils.

Cakkilyar Buddhist Tradition

At the time of the emergence of Buddhism, the Aruntatiyars who joined Buddhism were called 'Cākyā' in Buddhist terms and were registered in Pali as 'Cakkalā'. As Mahayana Buddhism was dying out, the Brahmin seers began to denigrate the word 'Cakkalā' by adding the Sanskrit word 'Cakkuḻi', which means one who eats the meat of a dead cattle, to the Pali word Cakkalā, and started calling them Cakkili, Cakkiliyar. Ezhil Ilangovaṉ thinks that this is the Buddhist caste name of the Cakkiliyar.

Buddhamithiran presents the argument that the word 'Cakkiliyar' is a Pali word and is a Tamil translation of the word Cākyā, and that there are one crore and twenty-five lakh people who are called by that name. This is the first evidence that Cakkiliyars are Buddhists. He also considers the word 'Cakkiliyar' to be a word of liberation, a great history that has been dormant for more than 2,500 years and it is waking up today. There is a clan called 'Mukkāyaṉuvāṟu' in Cakkiliyar. They are considered to be the ones who spread the teachings of Buddhist philosophy such as *Tam'mam*, *Puttam* and *Caṅkamam* all over the world. There is a clan among Cakkiliyar called 'Pōtivāṟu' which means those who considered the Pōti tree as sacred and followed the Buddha under the Pōti tree. Buddhamithiran places on record in his article that a scholar from the American Columbia University is trying to publish a well-researched document along with oral evidence about 'Cakkiliyars' are/were Buddhists'. In addition to this, many colleagues from Jawaharlal Nehru University, New Delhi are working on this project.

Vedic History of Aruntatiyars

A book titled *Vashista Vamsam* (2019) which explains the Vedic history of the Aruntatiyars of Tamil Nadu with relevant sources has recently been published by Sri Arunthathiyar Public Welfare Trust in Karamadai, Coimbatore district. In this book its author Chaturvedi Sadadanar says that 'Aruntatiyar' is not a caste name and that Aruntatiyars are the sons of Aruntati Devi who was the queen of Rājariṣi Vaṣiṣṭā. He identifies the Aruntatiyar as the Gurus (21), the Ayyars (22) as the Rājavamcas (30).

Aruntatiyars' Spiritual History

The histories written so far suggest that the Aruntatiyars have no distinct and honourable history. But Chaturvedi Catāṉaṉār has identified that the ancient history of Aruntatiyars is found in the ancient Vedas, Upanishads and epics like Mahabharata and Ramayana. (2019 : 117).

The entire Aruntatiyar social history has been restored by documenting the spiritual history of Aruntatiyar by Chaturvedi (2019), the movement history by Ezhil Iḷangovaṉ (2008), and the political history by Marc (2001).

Cakkilyars are Shaivites

The forefathers of the Cakkilyars, a sect of the Aruntatiyars, built and worshipped in Shiva temples. They are pure Shaivites who do not eat meat. There are evidences of Cakkilyars living even in the last century with 'Nāmam' [the religious mark on the forehead of the Vaishnavites] on their foreheads and 'koṇṭai' (bun) on their heads. So it is more likely that all the Cakkilyars were Shaivites and Vaishnavites.

Chapter - 3

Migrant Aruntatiyars,

Constructing Aruntatiyars' History through Oral Tradition

"Oral history breaks the assumption that written history is the only correct and reliable one. Oral history is more reliable than written history", says Marc (2001: 33). Inscriptions, archeological sources, travelogues and documents form the basic sources for writing history. It was N. Vaṉamamalai who advanced the anthropological theory that the community through which the messages of the vernacular can be understood can be understood through the oral language. Oral traditions serve as mirrors of the society that reflect the lives of the people of the respective times.

In the Tamil region, these caste groups are known by many names such as Cakkilyar, Mātāri, Mātikā, Pakaṭai, Tōṭṭi, Tom'maṉ, Cem'māṉ, Āti āntirā, Āti karnāṭakā, Mātiyavar, Muṟacār, Aruntatiyar and prefer to be called by the name 'Aruntatiyar'. They say that all other names other than Aruntatiyar are names given to them by the dominant caste and that these names are degrading to them and hence they do not want to be called by these names. The name Cakkili can be divided into Cakku + Kili = Cakkili. 'Kili' means fear. It means that those who are afraid of blows are Cakkiliyars.

The job of the dice is to play the game of the dominant caste in the game of life. They cannot act on their own. That is why they got this name, say the Aruntatiyars. The word dice can also mean to cheat cleverly. This could mean that the dice players are cleverly cheating. Some Aruntatiyars think that it can mean a completely different angle. They say that it can also mean that the dice act cleverly and deceive. The name 'Pakaṭai' is a name used not only in Tamil Nadu but also in the territories of Bangladesh and Pakistan outside India. 'Pakaṭai' or 'Pakaṭi' are the terms used to refer to the turban worn by men on their heads on special days. The Aruntatiyars say that they are also held in great esteem. 'Tōṭṭi' is another name for Aruntatiyars. The groups of people who carry out the task of announcing the news to the village public through Taṇṭōrā (tom-tom) are called Tōṭṭi. It is said that when the people of 'Mātikā' from undivided Andhra migrated to Tamil Nadu, the name 'Mātikā' underwent mutation such as Mātiyar, Mātāri, and Mātiyavar.

History of Aruntatiyars in Literatures and Dictionaries

The sources of the ancient history of the Tamil people and kings are the *Pattuppāṭṭu*, *Eṭṭuttokai* and other epics. References to 'Aruntatiyar', the root word of Aruntatiyar, are found in Sangha literatures such as *Akanāṉūṟu*, *Paripāṭal*, *Kalittokai*, *Aiṅkuṟunūṟu*, *Patiṟṟuppattu*, *Puṟanāṉūṟu*, *Tirikaṭukam, Perumpāṇāṟṟuppaṭai*, *Cīvakacintāmaṇi* and *Cilappatikāram*.

Devaneyan says that the Aruntatiyars are Parampars. In his *Tamiḻar Varalāṟu* (History of Tamils), he explains the word 'Parampan' as "people who do leather work and lime-stone burning". He also says that it is a Tamil clan that cobbles shoes. Devaneyan also believes that these people live in Tirunelveli, Madurai and Pudukkottai districts of Tamil Nadu.

At that time, sandals/shoes were made only of leather, so the meaning of leather worker can be considered correct. On the contrary, there is no place to assume that he is a leather worker.

Although Aṟampaṭavuraikārar, one of the commentators of *Cilappatikāram* confirms that Aruntatiyars are termed as 'Cemmār', Ezhil Iḷangovaṉ refers to Aṭiyārkku Nallār Aruntatiyar as 'Parampar'. Apitāṉa Cintāmaṇi also refers to Aruntatiyar as 'Parampan'. The 'Cemmārs' are considered to be agricultural migrant Tamils. Evidences from Tamil literary works show that the Cemmārs as the least numerous of the oppressed castes living in Tamil Nadu. They are also believed to have lived by hunting wild animals such as red deer and eating their meat and selling their skins.

Historical Evidences of Aruntatiyars

Most of the Aruntatiyars speak Telugu as their mother tongue and some speak Kannada as their mother tongue. Based on this, there is an opinion that they may have migrated to Tamil Nadu from Andhra Pradesh and Karnataka. In his book *Castes and Tribes of Southern India*, Edgar Thurston says that they must have migrated from Telugu or Kannada-speaking states. Leather workers in Tamil Nadu are considered to be at the bottom of the social hierarchy. There is a huge difference between Paṟaiyars and Aruntatiyars. Though these Aruntatiyars are Shaivites, they only worship female deities. They hold the plant Āvāram Ceṉṉā (Cassia Auriculata) in high esteem. Men of this caste are indiscriminate drinkers of intoxicating liquor. People who eat meat of all kinds of animals like pig, cow, etc. Women belonging to this caste are considered to be very beautiful. Cakkiliyars do not worship Mātaṅki, the special deity of the Mātikās. They worship Maturaivīraṉ, Māriyam'maṉ, Muṉīsvaraṉ, Tiraupati and Kaṅkammā. Thurston thinks that some Cakkiliyars styled themselves as Pakaṭaiyar, Mātāri and Raṇavīraṉ.

Rev. Father Marc, who has done an ethnographic study of the Aruntatiyars, suggests that all the Aruntatiyars in Tamil Nadu must have come to Tamil Nadu from Telugu and Kannada-speaking regions. The following are the historical notes recorded by him in his book *Aruntatiyar Vāḻum Varalāṟu,* (Marc, 2001: 8-10).

It seems that the first Telugu speakers came to Tamil Nadu during the Kākkatiyā Empire. The Kākkatiyā Empire was created by those who were petty kings under the later Cōḻās and Cālukkiyās.

The most important king in this empire in the thirteenth century was Piratāpa Rutrā (1295-1322). He ruled with Warangal in Andhra Pradesh as his capital. In the fourteenth century he came to Tiruchirappalli in Tamil Nadu and conquered parts of Tamil Nadu. Telugus may have settled in Tamil Nadu during this period.

Telugu-speaking people migrated to Tamil Nadu during Kriṣṇatēvarāyā's time as well. During the reign of Kriṣṇatēvarāyā (1509-1529) as the Vijayanagara Empire, he sent the general Nākam'mā Nāyakkar to the Pāṇṭiyā country to establish his dominance in Tamil Nadu. When Nākam'mā Nāyakkar was marching towards Madurai with his Vijayanagara forces, a group from Kampiḷi, a part of Vijayanagara, accompanied these forces. This group prepared food, clothing, milk, butter, and other supplies for the troops of Vijayanagara. This group is called 'Kampaḷattār'. During their stay and due to their occupation in Tamil Nadu, they were called 'Nine Kampaḷattār'. Aruntatiyars are also included in this 'Nine Kampaḷattār'. They may have come and stayed in this area.

Commander Nākammā Nāyakkar did not bow down to Kriṣṇatēvarāyā. As a result, Kriṣṇatēvarāyā sent a large force to Tamil Nadu under the command of his son Visvanāta Nāyakkar. He ruled Madurai from 1529 to 1564, during which a large number of Telugus came and settled in the region, possibly with the Aruntatiyars.

During the period of Nāyakkar kings, they offered human sacrifice while building temples, dams and bridges. For this it was customary to imprison and sacrifice Cakkiliyars who were considered inferior. Fearing for their lives, they fled to the southern part of the country. Those who fled stayed in Virudhunagar and Tirunelveli Districts. And Kampaḷattār who were unwilling to give wives to Mohammedans migrated to Tamil Nadu overnight. There is also a historical reference that Aruntatiyars were among those who migrated to Tamil Nadu.

"The Cakkiliyar is from one of the lower castes. There is no mention of them in early Tamil literature.They seem to have from the Telugu and Kannada regions. Though now Tamil-speaking people, their earlier mother tongue was Telugu or Kannada. Perhaps they came to Tamil Nadu in wake of the Vijayanagara invaders. They are workers on leather. It is their duty to remove the dead cattle from villages, in return the Cakkiliyars have to supply leather for agricultural purposes. A peculiar feature is that in the Madurai District the men of the Cakkiliyar caste belong to the right hand caste while the women belong to the left" (K. K. Pillai, 1979: 61). Thus, it can be known that Telugus came to Tamil Nadu from many parts of Andhra Pradesh at various times and for various reasons.

Kannadigas have come to Tamil Nadu like Telugus. By the thirteenth century, the Hōycālā Empire had spread over Mysore and its surrounding areas. Tuvāra Camuttiram was the capital of this Hōycālā Empire. Naracim'mā II (1220-1238) defeated the Pallavās and Pāṇṭiyās in battle. His son Kōmēsvaraṉ remained in office till 1267. His kingdom extended up to Kaṇṇaṉūr Kuppam, which is now known as Camayapuram, near Srīraṅkam. He divided his kingdom into two and gave it to his younger son Rāmanātaṉ (1254-1295). Rāmanātaṉ ruled Tamil Nadu from Kaṇṇaṉūr Kuppam. During his time, Aruntatiyars came to Tamil Nadu along with other Kannada speakers.

Then the Mohammedans invaded Tamil Nadu. They conquered and ruled Tamil Nadu. Hyder Ali and Tipu Sultan, who ruled Mysore, had invaded up to Palakkad. When he came, Kannada-speaking Aruntatiyars were brought with him as soldiers and to make hides for the horses. The reign of these Mohammedan kings extended up to Virutunakar District in Tamil Nadu. Kannada-speaking Aruntatiyars probably came to Virudhunagar district in Tamil Nadu during this period. The above-mentioned historical notes by Father Marc are about the Aruntatiyars in Vembakkottai, Sivakasi, Sattur, Srivilliputhur, Rajapaḷaiyam, Vathirayiruppu in Virudhunagar district, Tamil Nadu.

But it has also been recorded that the Aruntatiyar people who speak Tamil as their native language are still present in the undivided North Arcot and South Arcot Districts. (M.A. Krishnamurthy, 2006, pp. 26-27). To substantiate this point, Ezhil Iḷangovan̲ has stated that Aruntatiyars did not come from Andhra Pradesh or Karnataka; rather they were natives of Tamil Nadu.

History of Aruntatiyars marked on the Inscriptions

There is an opinion that the Cakkilyars settled in Tamil Nadu only during the time of Kriṣṇatēvarāyā (1509-1529) i.e. in the sixteenth century. But there are inscriptional evidences of Cakkiliyars living in Tamil Nadu before the sixteenth century. They are well documented periodically.

There is a lake called 'Periya Cakkilicci Ēri' (Periya Cakkilicci Lake) at Ketta Nayakan̲puthur on the way from Danish Pettai to Ramamurthy Nagar in Salem District. There are two inscriptions near a dam on its banks. They are inside the lake. The slum people of that village worship them as two female deities named Periya Campammā and Cin̲n̲a Campammā. Both the stones are placed on the eighth century inscription. Text of those two inscriptions begin with

'ஸ்ரீ கிடங்கல் //Srī kiṭaṅkaḷ//

புலியார் மகனல்லி //Puliyār makanalli//

ஓட்டை கண்டது' //Ōṭṭai kaṇṭatu//

Some rare facts are revealed from the text of this inscription. The old name of the lake was 'Srī Kiṭaṅkaḷ'. Kiṭaṅkaḷ refers to water level. A person called Nalli has put a dam in it. Mataku (dam) has a hole. Nalli's father's name is Puliyār. It can be considered that this great son belongs to that clan as Cakkilyar worship it as their deity till date. It is also clear that the lake dates back to the eighth century as the dam is reported to have been built. Based on the references of Aruntatiyars in Tamil inscriptions, it can be concluded that Aruntatiyars were the original inhabitants of Tamil Nadu.

There is a hill called 'Sakkili Durgam' which is a part of Senjikottai in Vilupuram. It is made of natural ramparts. It is possible that 'Cantirakiri Fort', named after the Aruntatiyar King named Chandragiri, was later called 'Senjikottai'. The inscription 'Sakkili Durgam' on the facade of the fort confirms this information.

There are some epigraphical evidences of the Aruntatiyars who have lived in Tamil Nadu in the eleventh and twelfth centuries. The Risabeshvarar temple inscription at Sengam in Tiruvannamalai District contains the following lines. All the castes, including Niyātars and twelve Paṇimakkaḷs, the Vēṭars, the Pāṇars, the Paṟaimutalis, the Cekkilis, the Iruḷars, and all the other castes, with Antaṇaṉ as the head of the learned clans. (South Indian Inscription, Vol. 7, p. 49). The date of this inscription is 1258 AD.

The Tiruvannamalai Inscription

> 'ஜொம்மண்ண உடையார் மகமை மக்க திரை கார்த்திகை பாடி உள்ளபும் ... நாட... நாய் ஆடு திரை தாம ... கை தெண்டம் உண்டிகை எ... யும்... காணிபட்டு நார் எண்ணெய் நால் எருது நார் பசு நால் எருமை நளி... ந்த... தாகு இரும்பு ... சக்கிலித்திரை ...வெற்றிலை... மை மற்றுமும் ஊர்...பா...காணிக்கயும் சர்வ மானியம் ஆக'.

//Pacu viṭukaiyālum aintalai maṇiyiṭukaiyālum mekaṭukukaikku **cakkilikku** tericaṉam kāṭṭi tolālē ceyta tiruvaṭi nilaikku mekaṭukukaikku pattukku pota cempoṉ arukaḻañcuyiṭukaiyālum[1]// (South Indian Inscription, Vol. 7, p. 68). The year mentioned in this inscription is 1202 AD.

A Tamil inscription at Kaivara in Cintāmaṇi taluka of Kolar District bordering Tamil Nadu in Karnataka mentions as follows.

---

1. It was felt that this particular passage was untranslatable. As a result, the translator would like to point out that this inscription mentions the word '**cakkili**' and this word has been written in bold letters.

'ஜொம்மண்ண உடையார் மகமை மக்க திரை கார்த்திகை பாடி உள்ளயும் ... நாட... நாய் ஆடு திரை தாம ... கை தெண்டம் உண்டிகை எ... யும்... காணிபட்டு நார் எண்ணெய் நால் எருது நார் பசு நால் எருமை நளி... ந்த... தாகு இரும்பு ... சக்கிலித்திரை ...வெற்றிலை... மை மற்றுமும் ஊர்...பா...காணிக்கயும் சர்வ மானியம் ஆக'.

// jommaṉṉa uṭaiyār makimai mikka tiṟai kārttikai pāṭi uḷḷayum… nāṭa... nāy āṭu tirai tāma... kāy teṇṭam uṇṭikai e… yum… kāṇippaṭṭu nār eṇṉey nāḷ itu ṉār pacu nāḷ erumai naḷi… nta… tāku irumpu … **cakkiḷittirai** …. veṟṟilai ... maiy māṟṟamum ūr... pā... kāṇikkaiyum carva māṉiyam āka[1]// (Epigraphy of Carnatika vol.10) The year mentioned in this inscription is 1374 AD. This inscription confirms that the word 'Cakkilittirai' was in use in Tamil Nadu in the fourteenth century.

Another inscription found in Tiruvannamalai mentions the following information:

'...செப்பத்தத்துக்கு துணை நிலமாக இட்ட கிழன் மேலாய்க் கிடக்கும் வாவைக்கும் வடக்கில் நாலடியில் கிழைவாவையில் கீழ்வரம்புக்கு வடக்கும் மெல்பார்க்கெல்லை வடக்கின் நாலடியர் வடவரம்புக்கும் சக்கிலியன் குண்டிலுக்கும் பெருநான் கெல்லை நத்தத்தில் நாறுகாலுக்குக் கிழக்கும் வடபார்க்கெல்லை...'

//…ceppattukku tuṇai nilamāka iṭṭa kiḻāṉ mēlāy kiṭakkum vāvaikkum vaṭakkil nālaṭiyil kiḻaivāaiyil kīḻvarampukku vaṭakkum melpāṟkkellaiyvaṭakkiṉ nālaṭiyār vaṭavarampukkum **cakkiliyaṉ** kuṇṭilukkum perunāṉ kellai nattattil ṉāṟukālukku kiḻakkum vaṭapāṟkkellai…[2]// (South Indian Inscription, Vol. 8, p. 36). The date of this inscription is 1030 AD.

Jeyavīratēvaṉ has recorded another epigraphical evidence about Cakkiliyar in his book *Ceruppu* (2010: 27)]. It is a later period of Cōḻā inscription. The following is mentioned in the inscription: //eṉakku cari iṉṉāta **cakkiliyaṉ** ceruppum eṭuttu tampalamum tiṉṟavaṉāvēṉ//[3]

'In the year following Kulōttuṅkaṉ I's reign, i.e. 1071, the second year of his reign, there was a great struggle, melee, and riot

1. For the same reason mentioned in the footnote no. 2.
2. Same reason as mentioned in the footnote no. 2.
3. Same reason as mentioned in the footnote no. 2.

between 'Valaṅkai' (right-handed faction was made up of castes with an agricultural basis) and 'Iṭaṅkai' (left-handed faction was made of metal workers, weavers, etc) in the Prahmatēya Brahmin villages of RājamākēntiraCaturvēti Maṅkaḷam, located in today's Pāpanācam and Naṉṉilam areas, which were called Nitta Viṉōta Vaḷanāṭu. It has been mentioned that Paṟaiyar of Valaṅkai division and Aruntatiyar and Paḷḷar of Iṭaṅkai division participated in this protest. In 1091, during the reign of Kulōttuṅkaṉ I, an inscription says that a similar fight took place between Valaṅkai and Iṭaṅkai. The Āṭuturai inscription says that the 98 castes of the Valaṅkai and the 98 castes of the Iṭaṅkai joined forces to oppose the dominance of the Veḷḷāḷars and Brahmins. The inscription says that 'when Valaṅkai and Iṭaṅkai made a pact in Vaṭapāti Maṅkaḷam and fought against the government, they were oppressed and left the village'. This inscription is found in Tiruvarangam temple. (Ezhil Ilangovaṉ, 2002: 37-38).

The earliest of the above inscriptions is dated 1030 AD. The inscription mentions that the name of a particular place is given as 'Cakkiliyaṉ kuṇṭil. From the fact that a place was given such a name, we can know for sure that Cakkiliyars lived in Tamil Nadu long before that period. An inscription of the Cōḻā period indicates that Paṟaimutalis, Cakkilimutalis, Kaikkōlmutalis and Veḷḷāḷamutalis were present in the village council.

In an inscription of Chengalpattu district dated 1397 AD, the phrase 'Cakkili Paṭṭaṟai' (Cakkili's workshop] is found (A. Sivasubramanian, 2017:7). This term refers to factories. This inscription confirms that Cakkiliyars of Tamil Nadu were owners of tanneries as early as the fourteenth century before the Nāyakkar rule (1529-1736).

History of Aruntatiyars on the Copperplate Inscriptions

Along with the inscriptional evidence that the Aruntatiyars were the original Tamils, there is also some evidence found in the inscriptions on the copper plates. In the Kalingarayaṉ Dam copperplate inscription published by S. Rasu in the book *Koṅku*

Vēḷāḷar Ceppētu Paṭṭayaṅkaḷ (Copperplates of *Koṅku Vēḷāḷar*), the following is found.

'To free Kocavaṉ, Kuṟavaṉ, Maṟavaṉ, Vaḷaiyaṉ, Paṟaiyaṉ, Cakkiliyaṉ without tax, we have made a donation to the house of Paṭṭakar to bring to Paṭikkārar, the poets who have to go to Kārala Maṇikku Muṭavāṇṭi and Kurupāṇṭi'. (Copperplate inscription of Kongu Vellalar, p. 268). This inscription belongs to the fourteenth century (1374 AD).

The following lines are mentioned in the Ciṟuvalai Zamin copper plate found in Āṉaimalai, Coimbatore district.

சாலிய வாகன வறுசங்கள் ஆயிரத்து இருநூற்று நாற்பத்து அஞ்சாண்டு செல்வா நின்ற சருவசித்தி வையாசி சா தசமி ஆதவாறமும் உத்திர நஞ்சத் நட்சேத்திரமும் காலவாகற்ணமும் பிரமநாம யோகமும் யிப்படிக் கொற்ற சுபதினத்தில் அனுப்பச் சக்கிலியற் கொல்ல சக்கிலியற் மதுரை சக்கிலியற் கானக்காட்டுச் சக்கிலியற்யிந்த சக்கிலியச் சாதி அனவரில் ஆசாரத்தப்பான பேருக்குக் கவுறும் கொட்ட கோலும் கொடுத்து சாதியாசாறம் வளுவாமல் நடத்திவிக்கிக் கொள்ளும் படிக்கு சாதி அனவோரும் எழுதிக் குடுத்தி பட்டயம்'...

//cāliya vākaṉa varucaṅkaḷ āyirattu irunūṟṟu nāṟpattu añcāntu celvā niṉṟa caruvacitti vaiyāci cā tacami ātavāramum uttira nañcat naṭcattiramum kālvākarṇamum piramanāma yōkamum ippaṭi koṟṟa cupatiṉattil aṉuppa **cakkiliyar** koḷḷa **cakkiliyar** maturai **cakkiliyar** kāṇakkāṭṭu **cakkiliyar**yinta **cakkiliya** cāti aṉavariṉ ācārattappāṉa pērukku kavarum koṭṭa kōlum koṭuttu cātiyācāram valuvāmal naṭattivikki koḷḷum paṭikku cāti aṇavōrum eḻuti kuṭutti paṭṭayam//[1]

There are some lines in the Perur Dam copperplate inscription published in the Kongu National Community Documents published by S. Rasu. 'Oṉṉappa Kauṇṭar goes to Kōṉiyammaṉ Temple by taking the signatures of Mātāri which contain the details of the following members as per the copperplate given by Vatilu Mātāris to Oṉṉappa Kauṇṭar : Eṉṭa Pakaṭai, Māyapakaṭai, Vīrapakaṭai, Pāḻiya Pakaṭai, Pakaṭikkatti Pakaṭai, Vaṭṭika Pakaṭai, Mallika Pakaṭai, Pūvulu Pakaṭai, Ciṇṭūram Pakaṭai, Kal Pakaṭai, Kauri Pakaṭai, Karuci Pakaṭai, Vaṇṇa Kāriya Pakaṭai, Aṇṇāvi

1. Same reason as mentioned in the foot no. 2.

Pakaṭai, Kuliya Pakaṭai, Kunjali Pagadai (Kuñcali Pakaṭai). Uraikāra Pakaṭai, Kōkuli Pakaṭai, Pīraṅka Pakaṭai. In the year 1446, 96 castes appeared. Along with the lower clans like Paṟaiyar, Mātikā or Cakkiliyar, 98 castes are mentioned in the copperplate inscriptions of the Cōḻā Period (M.A. Krishnamurthy, 2006: 31).

History of Aruntatiyars according to Government Records and Manuals

There is a dam named 'Cakkiliyaṉ Aṇai' (Cakkiliyaṉ Dam) at the foothills of Kodaikkaṉal in the old Ayakkudi village of Dindigul District. The descendants of Cakkiliyar, who built the dam, are still known as 'Aṇaikaṭṭi kūṭṭam' (the group of people who built the dam). The irrigators using the water of the dam are still giving a part of their yield to them in the name of 'Aṇai Nel' (rice that is grown due to the constant supply of water from the dam). It is mentioned in the revenue department government record of West Ayakkudi village that 'Varadhamaṉadhi' water is stored by Cakkiliyar Dam and flows through the big canal [Veḷḷaikkutirai (Tamil magazine), p. 63).

The Madurai District Manual of 1868 says the following about the Cakkiliyars. 'They tan leather and manufacture sandals, saddles and leather goods.' These ethnic women have unique facial beauty and body structure and are well behaved. In Thanjavur District Manual of 1883, 'Cakkilyars' are regarded as the lowest caste. It has been said that these people who speak Telugu in some parts of the district and wear naaman (white mark worn on the forehead by the Vaishnavites) should be immigrants from Telugu areas. (Thurston, 2010: 4).

Near Senjikottai in Tiruvannamalai, there is a small hill. According to the oral narratives among the people of the area, during the reign of King Ceñci, the Aruntatiyar community lived in this mountain and made leather coins for their livelihood. The place where the people of the Aruntatiyar race lived is still known as 'Cakkiliyaṉ Kuṉṟu' (Cakkiliyaṉ Hillock) and 'Cakkiliyaṉ Malai' (Cakkiliyaṉ Hill).

It is worth noting here that a small village called 'Cakkiliyaṉ Kāni in Tiruppullaṇi taluka, Ramanathapuram District and a place called 'Cakkliyan Colony' near Vasudevanallur, Tirunelveli District, a village called 'Cakkilippaṭṭi' in Arur taluka of Dharmapuri District and a 'Cakkiliyan pond' in Avarangadu village in Ottappidaram taluka of Thuthukkudi District are still in existence. Thus, it can be known through inscriptions, copperplates and documents that the Aruntatiyars are the ancient inhabitants of Tamil Nadu.

Tamil Nadu's Aruntatiyars: Historical Reconstruction

Their historical reconstruction is an important element in the formation of society and castes. Reconstruction is the identification of deliberately hidden or distorted histories and uncovering their true nature. It is said that the mouth of history cannot be covered with a furnace lid. "Whatever is hidden in history is not like an old sandal that has been thrown away and never returned. Histories continue to unfold according to the needs and characteristics of the changing circumstances of the present. It will also make an explosive manifestation" said Louis Pierre Althusser, a French Marxist philosopher. Dr Ambedkar's position that 'whatever in society is wrongly settled is never settled and it has to be resettled' is worth recalling here.

The stories of the Aruntatiyars, the first anti-caste fighter Maduraiveeran, the first self-sacrificing Kuyili, the first freedom fighter Oṇṭivīraṉ, the Brahmin-turned-Muttupakaṭai Muttappaṉ, the Pāḷayakkār Nīlakaṇṭa Pakaṭai of the Pāpanācam area, the stories of the primitive Aruntatiyars are being recreated in the form of novels, dramas and research articles.

Chapter - 4

Unknown Pāḷaiyams of Aruntatiyars

Biased History

The Seventeenth to eighteenth century period is of various historical importance in the history of Tamil Nadu, especially in Southern Tamil Nadu. Many historical events that occurred during this period have been systematically recorded. The histories of the dominant castes such as Tirumalai Nāyakkar, Kaṭṭapommaṉ, Marutu brothers, Vēlunācciyār, Cētupati, Tīraṉ Ciṉṉamalai, Aruvā Vēlu have been elaborated with painstaking detail and exaggeration where necessary. On the other hand, historical records have already been recorded which systematically hide and distort the true histories of martyrs like Maturaivīraṉ, Kāttavarāyaṉ, Oṇṭivīraṉ, Muttaṉ Pakaṭai, Kantaṉ Pakaṭai, Veṇṇikkālāṭi, Ciṉṉakālāṭi, Periyakālāṭi, Ciṉṉacokkāṉ, Periyacokkāṉ, Kuṇatuṅkaṉ, Ciṉṉakōṭāri, Periyakōṭāri, Pōṭṭimuttāṉ, Nallamāṭaṉ, Ciṉṉavīriyaṉ, Periyaviriyaṉ from the Dalit community.

Southern Palayams - A Historical View

It was during Visvanāta Nāyakkar's time that the Pāḷaiyam system was introduced, and Poligars were also appointed. Palayam is also called 'Pāḷaiyappaṭṭu'. Poligars themselves later became Zamindars. Tirunelveli has a special name as Teṉṉāṭu. Tirunelveli was also a region known for famous Pāḷaiyams. Ciṅkampaṭṭi, Ūrkkāṭu, Ūttumalai, Vaṭakarai, Curaṇṭai, Naṭuvakkuṟicci, Kurukkalpaṭṭi, Aḻakāpuri, Neṟkaṭṭāṉ Cevvayal, Talaivaṉkōṭṭai, Tēṉmalai, Kollamkoṇṭāṉ, Cēttūr, Potikai Malai are known as the western part of Tirunelvēli district. These are also called 'Maṟavar

Pāḷaiyams' and 'Tamil̲ Pāḷaiyams'. Pāñcālaṅkur̲icci, Mēlamāntai, Kāṭalkuṭi and Kuḷattūr are the eastern districts of Tirunelvēli district. These are called 'Nāyakkar Pāḷaiyams' and 'Teluku Pāḷaiyams'. All the western Pāḷaiyams, the Mar̲avar Pāḷaiyams were situated as a unified region at the foothills of the Western Ghats. Ner̲kaṭṭān̲ Cevvayal in the west and Pāñcālaṅkur̲icci in the east were famous Pāḷaiyams.

Unknown Aruntatiyar Pāḷaiyams

Among the so-called Tamil̲ Pāḷaiyam, Ner̲kaṭṭān̲ Cevvayal and Potikai Malai were Arunatiyar Pāḷaiyams and later became Zamins. In the eighteenth century, Oṇṭivīran̲ Pakaṭai and Nīlakaṇṭa Pakaṭai were the chiefs of Ner̲kaṭṭān̲ Cevvayal and Podhigai Malai respectively. The headquarters of these regions, which were a unified region at the foothills of the Western Ghats, was Ner̲kaṭṭān̲ Cevvayal. It is significant to note here that Mathivannan̲ has pointed out in his interview that the explorers have mentioned that he created Singampatti Zamin after killing Neelakandan̲, who was the king of Potikai Malai region (Ul̲aippavar Āyutam, January - 2010:19). It is worth noting here that Subramaniya Kavirayar, who belongs to Singampatti, told N. Van̲amamalai that Nallakuṭṭi established the Singampatti estate after killing Neelakandan̲ and that the places called 'Neelakandan̲ Thalaivetti Parai' and 'Neelakandan̲ Kasam' are still there (Arunan, 2006:181-182). Also, it is worth recalling here that Dhin̲akaran̲'s (Tamil daily) Veḷḷimalai 'Regional News' has mentioned that Neelakanda Pagadai ruled the Pabanasam hill region.

The ancestral history of Oṇṭivīran̲, who built all the Tirunelveli Pāḷaiyam, and the history of Neelakanda Pagadai, who was the king of the famous Podhigai Malai region, have been deliberately distorted and hidden by the historians and the dominant caste people.

Aruntatiyar Pāḷaiyams in Northern Districts

The areas where the Aruntatiyars lived in the northern districts are often called 'Aruntatiyar Pāḷaiyam'. Over time, this situation changed and near the areas where the Aruntatiyars lived, the government built blockhouses called 'colony' for them. The pre-existing native Aruntatiyar areas and blockhouses have been mixed and renamed as Indira Colony, MGR Colony, Kamaraj Colony, and Kurinji Nagar. According to local people, there are still Aruntatiyar Pāḷaiyams in Poondhamalli in Chennai, Padunelli in Kanchipuram District and Komangalam Panchayat, Kalyāṇa Kuppam Panchayat in Tiruvaḷḷūr District, Ayyāppaṭṭi Panchayat of Tiruvannamalai District.

Ethnohistory of Neṟkaṭṭāṉ Cevvayal Pāḷaiyam

About ten kilometres north-west of Sankarankovil in Tirunelveli District and about five kilometres to the east of Vasudevanallur is Cevvayal, a small village with fertile land and a large water table around it. The place was also called Neṟkaṭṭum Cevvayal Fort. Located in Arināṭu, one of the 22 forts of the Pāṇṭiyā Kings, Neṟkaṭṭum Cevvāyāl is the center of the 'Pañcataḷam' (five regions) of Tēvatāṉam, Caṅkaraṉkōvil, Tārukāpuram, Tēṉmalai and Karivalamvantanallūr. Cakkilyars were the Aruntatiyars who cleared the dense forest and turned it into arable land. A man named Iruḷappa Piḷḷai, who belonged to the dominant caste living in the area, fraudulently appropriated the rich farmland from them. The Cakkiliyars appealed to Pūlittēvar, who was guarding the surrounding areas of Āvuṭaiyārpuram, to get their land back. Pūlittēvar recovered the rich lands lost to Iruḷappa Piḷḷai and handed them back to Cakkiliyars. During this event, Pūlittēvar saw the miracle of a rabbit driving away a dog in the area and was amazed to know the rare power of the area. Besides, Pūlittēvar also built a new fort at the same place. The site of the fort became Neṟkaṭṭāṉ Cevvayal and the headquarters of Pūlittēvar. This is corroborated by the copperplates of the Pūlittēvar's period that 'they changed the capital of their ancestors from the capital to Āvuṭaiyārpuram and built a fort at Neṟkaṭṭum Cevvāyāl and ruled from this place as their capital'. It was known as Neṟkaṭṭum Cevvāyāl Pāḷaiyam during Nāyakkar reign and Neṟkaṭṭum (one who agreed to pay tax) Cevvayal Zamin during British rule. Until then, rice was collected as tax and because of the refusal to pay tax, it was changed to 'Neṟkaṭṭāṉ (one who refused to pay tax) Cevvayal' and it is still given under the same name. Due to his insatiable rage against Pūlittēvar, the British destroyed Neṟkaṭṭāṉ Cevvayal Fort and razed it to the ground. Even the name of the town called 'Neṟkaṭṭāṉ Cevvayal' where Pūlittēvar lived was changed to 'Āvuṭaiyārpuram'.Thus, the British resolved their animosity by an act of revenge. Caldwell has recorded this news in his book '*Tirunelveli District*'. This Neṟkaṭṭāṉ Cevvayal was not only the Pāḷaiyam of Aruntatiyar but also a famous Zamin.

Ethnohistory of Āvuṭaiyārpuram Pāḷaiyam

Due to the severe drought in Rāmanātapuram in Tamil Nadu in the seventeenth century and after a great riot among the Maṟavars of the area, the ancestors of Pūlittēvar, the first Citraputra Tēvaṉ, left the Rāmanātapuram area and searched for survival in a place called Āvuṭaiyārpuram near Neṟkaṭṭāṉ Cevvayal in Tirunelvēli District. They built a new fort at a different place and called the area 'Putukkōṭṭai' as they gathered together as a family and lived together to gain fame. After Citraputra Tēvar I (1610-1638), Kātappā Pūlittēvaṉ III (1638-1663) and Citraputra Tēvar II (1663-1726) ruled the Āvuṭaiyārpuram Pāḷaiyam. After them, Kātappā Pūlittēvaṉ IV (1726-1767) became the head of the Āvuṭaiyārpuram Fort and Pāḷaiyam. As per the historical records it is Pūlittēvaṉ who fought against the British.

Āvuṭaiyārpuram Pāḷaiyam is famous for its history dating back a thousand years. Madurai also served as a Pāḷaiyam which paid tax to the Nāyakkars. At first it was inhabited for a long time and then it disappeared. Then it continued again during the reign of Nākammanāyakkaṉ Visvanāta Nāyakkar. This 'Āvuṭaiyārpuram is one of the seventy-two Pāḷaiyam's established by Visvanāta Nāyakkar and is a historic Pāḷaiyam' (N. Rācaiyā, 2005 : 59 - 60). T. B. Pandian in his book *The slaves of the soil in southern India* (1893:3) writes about the news of Āvuṭaiyārpuram Zamin in Tirunelvēli, which was once under the control of Cakkiliya king. When the Pāḷaiyams were abolished and turned into Zamins, the Zamin of Āvuṭaiyārpuram was also called Neṟkaṭṭāṉ Cevvayal Zamin.

Chapter - 5

Aruntatiyars in the Indian War of Independence

Reconstructing the history of oppressed communities with the help of folk literature such as folk songs, folk ballads, oral expressions, etc. is more legitimate than seeing it from written histories. In that way, the history of the Aruntatiyars, the Dalit people of Tamil Nadu, is constructed through folk songs, ballads and oral stories. This article is an attempt to find out the social history and cultural roots of Cakkiliyars through the stories collected from *Talit Kataippāṭalkaḷ* (*Dalit Folk Ballads*) (2010).

Oṇṭivīraṉ, the son of the soil - Historiography

In some parts of eighteenth-century Tamil Nadu, the Pakaṭais (The castes mentioned in the Schedule list variously known as Cakkiliyar, Mātāri, Pakaṭai identify themselves as Arunatiyar; This initiative was started during the colonial rule itself) were Poligars [Each Poligar was considered the owner of a territory or Pāḷaiyam (province/region)] and Zamindars. This village Neṟkaṭṭāṉ Cevvayal was also owned by Pakaṭais. About ten kilometres north-west of Caṅkaraṉkōvil town in Tirunelvēli District and about five kilometres east of Vasudevanallur is a fertile earthy Neṟkaṭṭāṉ Cevvayal with a plateau, a large water table and arable fields. He used to live with a contemporary named Kātappatturai alias Pūlittēvar, who was in charge of his land, as his close friend.

Oṇṭivīraṉ also got married to his uncle's daughter Vīram'mā. When Oṇṭivīraṉ's father died, he took over the responsibility of the region. He came along with his friend and contemporary Pūlittēvar. When the Zamin system was changed to Pāḷaiyam, Pūlittēvar, who was guarding the northern part of the village, took charge of the Pāḷaiyam due to chicaneries and fraudulent practices of Iruḷappa Piḷḷai, various scandalous events related to caste atrocities and manipulations that were happening in Tamil Nadu, and the increase in population of his community people. Oṇṭivīraṉ and Pūlittēvaṉ ruled Pāḷaiyam together. Oṇṭivīraṉ also held the additional responsibility of the Force Commander. Oṇṭivīraṉ singlehandedly led the war against the enemy.

In this situation, the politically astute British provided military assistance to the Nawab of Arcot and thereby took the responsibility of collecting taxes from the Pāḷaiyams. In 1755, Oṇṭivīraṉ and Pūlittēvaṉ protested why they should pay taxes to the British. They camped in an area called Tēṉmalai under the leadership of the British commander Heron to wage war on Neṟkaṭṭāṉ Cevvayal because they refused to pay taxes to foreigners.

Oṇṭivīraṉ went into the camp alone, took the sword, horse and flag in order to break the oath of the British, turned the cannon towards their camp and rushed towards Neṟkaṭṭāṉ Cevvayal after hurling Nākarā (musical instrument played to announce the war). He earned the name Oṇṭivīraṉ (Oṇṭi + vīraṉ = Oṇṭivīraṉ - 'Oṇṭi' single person and 'Vīraṉ' brave person) because he went on as a single person and won the challenge. Later, the forces led by Oṇṭivīraṉ marched out and defeated the Heron's army. Later, in 1756 and 1757, Oṇṭivīraṉ again faced another battlefield.

The Southern Pāḷaiyams (to collect taxes for the king and help in war, a block of villages left in charge of a chief) of Tirunelvēli, including Eṭṭayapuram Pāḷaiyam, were seen as tarnishing the spirit of freedom in the then Tirunelvēli region. Oṇṭivīraṉ and Pūlittēvaṉ won the battle over those Pāḷaiyams. Oṇṭivīraṉ mobilised the support of the Tamil camps against the whites through such raids.

As Āḻvārkuṟicci Aḻakappaṉ was working in favour of the British. Oṇṭivīraṉ went with his army and defeated Aḻakappaṉ and captured him. When Marutanāyakam came to attack Oṇṭivīraṉ, Oṇṭivīraṉ escaped with his commander Veṇṇikkālāṭi and came to Cevvayal.

On 2nd July 1759, Marutanāyakam went with a large force and captured the other armed troops of Ūttumalai and Curaṇṭai. Oṇṭivīraṉ went and recovered them with a large force on 6th November of the same year. Enraged, Marutanāyakam along with Toṇṭaimāṉ's army attacked Vācutēvanallūr. Oṇṭivīraṉ and Pūlittēvaṉ went in two separate armies with about 3000 soldiers and won the battle which lasted for twenty days.

On May 13, 1767, the force led by British commander Donald Campbell attacked Neṟkaṭṭāṉ Cevvayal. Realising the situation, Pūlittēvaṉ went into hiding. Oṇṭivīraṉ was on the battlefield. In the end, Pūlittēvaṉ went to the Āvuṭai Nācciyār temple in Caṅkaraṉkōvil and went into hiding, fearing the British, and never came out. Its mystery has not been unraveled till date. After the death of Pūlittēvaṉ, Oṇṭivīraṉ again took charge of the camp and took care of Pūlittēvaṉ's children. He won the battles of Kaḷakkāṭu, Kaṅkaikoṇṭāṉ Tiruvilliputtūr and Putukkōṭṭai. In the final battle of Tēnmalai, the great warrior Oṇṭivīraṉ died on the battlefield.

Eventually, the Thevar communities, who had settled from many towns, became the majority of Neṟkaṭṭāṉ Cevvayal, and the natives, the Aruntatiyars and the Paṟaiyars, became a minority and landless as they died in large numbers in the battlefield. Later they migrated to many towns like Muṉār, Kōvilpaṭṭi, Tūttukkuṭi and Tirunelvēli to survive the famine. The rest were made to resettle in the eastern part of Neṟkaṭṭāṉ Cevvayal village at a place called 'Paccēri'. They were also excluded from entering the village.

Oṇṭivīraṉ is still worshipped by the people of Kaṭalāṭi, the native town of Pūlittēvaṉ. The Aruntatiyars also worship Oṇṭivīraṉ as their family deity and as an idol in the towns of Pacuvantaṉai,

Kuruvikuḷam and Paruttikkuḷam. Oṇṭivīraṉ lived as a Zamindar, chief of Pāḷaiyam, king and army commander.

Oṇṭivīraṉ in Folk Ballads

When a story about a particular hero is narrated in the form of a song in conjunction with several historical events, it becomes a historical narrative. In that way, Oṇṭivīraṉ, who troubled the British, Arcot Nawab and Khan Sahib Yusuf Khan in the field at the beginning of the Indian freedom struggle, belonged to the Pakaṭai clan. Oṇṭivīraṉ's heroic story is available in the form of historical ballads, Kummi (a dance performed by women moving around to the tune of the song they are singing and clapping), Cintu (a type of musical song composed of four beats of seven to nine syllables), Play and Villuppāṭṭu (a folk performance performed by singing the story and reciting interspersed verses while tapping a bell-shaped bow-shaped instrument with a stick). 'Oṇṭivīraṉ's Ballads', 'Oṇṭivīraṉ's Villuppattu', *Oṇṭivīraṉ:* Tāḻnta Kulattiṉ Taḷapati [A Commander of a 'Lowly Clan' (play in Tamil)] are featured separately in the titles *Pūlittēvaṉ Cintu* and *Pūlittēvaṉ Kum'mi* and the folk ballads about Oṇṭivīraṉ are featured as sub-stories.

There are some subtle differences between the stories collected in the field study of Oṇṭivīraṉ and the stories narrated in Pūlittēvaṉ folk ballads about Oṇṭivīraṉ. It is recorded in the history of Pūlittēvaṉ that Neṟkaṭṭāṉ Cevvayal was Maṟavar Pāḷaiyam which was situated near Vācutēvanallūr, northwest of Caṅkaraṉkōvil and that Pūlittēvaṉ was its head. But in fact the ancestors of Oṇṭivīraṉ were the real landholders of Neṟkaṭṭum Cevvayal area and Oṇṭivīraṉ was the leader of the same camp in the change of time. In one of the Oṇṭivīraṉ folk ballads, we find in the following panegyric lines:

"The mind will be moved and cooled down

Neṟkaṭṭum Cevvayal!

In this beautiful village!

Aruntatiyars lived since time immemorial

As owners of these lands.

They lived by farming.

By owning farmlands

They lived in luxury

Like a Zamindar."

[*Talit Kataippāṭalkaḷ* (Dalit Folk Ballads, 2010, p. 29)]

When South Tamil Nadu was divided into various Pāḷaiyams during the Nāyakkar regime, Ne̱rkaṭṭum and Cevvayal became a Pāḷaiyam. The following lines from Dalit Folk Ballads reveal such information:

"When the Pāḷaiyam system prevailed

Ne̱rkaṭṭāṉ Cevvayal Pāḷaiyam

Changed under the leadership

Of the Protector (Oṇṭivīraṉ)!"

[*Talit Kataippāṭalkaḷ* (Dalit Folk Ballads, 2010, p. 38)]

The true history has been distorted due to the fact that there are no inscriptions, copperplates or palm leaf manuscripts among the illiterate Aruntatiyar people. This may be a conspiracy by the dominant caste to keep the Aruntatiyar community under their control. In addition to the insidious usurpation of Pāḷaiyam leadership, the trick of enslaving real Pāḷaiyam victims by appointing them as officers and servants has also occurred in written history.

Oṇṭivīraṉ, the son of the soil - A Historical Restoration

This chapter tries to establish that Oṇṭivīraṉ of Ne̱rkaṭṭāṉ Cevvayal Pāḷaiyam is the Oṇṭivīraṉ of Cevvayal Pāḷaiyam through the 'Oṇṭivīraṉ Folk Ballads' collected in the field research conducted in Tirunelvēli district as an attempt to restore the history of Oṇṭivīraṉ who belongs to the Pakaṭai tribe through one of the folk ballads.

The seventeenth and eighteenth centuries can be considered as a period when various historically significant events and incidents were taking place in India, especially in Southern Tamil Nadu, and great changes were taking place in the social, economic, political and cultural fields. In some parts of Tamil Nadu during these centuries, Aruntatiyars were large and small landowners, warriors, peasants and zamindars.

The Poligar system, introduced during the Nāyakkar reign, was abolished after the creation of the Madras Presidency by the British in 1803. All the Pāḷaiyams were destroyed but in course of time they evolved into Zamin system. Poligars acquired the status of Zamindars. Robert Caldwell (2004:171) describes the Zamindars as the descendants of the Poligars, meaning 'Poligars live with us in the form of Zamindars as peaceful successors'.

Oṇṭivīraṉ's Early Life

Oṇṭivīraṉ was born in 1710 AD as the son of Pettavīraṉ and Vīrammā in that Zamindar family. At an early age, he learned to fight with swords, do fencing with a staff, ride horses, play drums, sing, weave, and work with leather. The folk ballad speaks of it thus:

"At the age of twelve
He learnt to do all kinds of adventures
He learnt swordsmanship
He also learnt horse riding with perfection!
He learnt how to beat the drum and sing
He also learnt meticulously
The leather work that
Which is his hereditary profession."
[*Talit Kataippāṭalkaḷ* (Dalit Folk Ballads, 2010, p. 31)]

The *Pūlittēvaṉ Kum'mi Song* records the heroic deeds of Oṇṭivīraṉ as follows:

"I will peel the skin and cut off the tail
I will beautify leather good
I will also sew the scabbard
I will wait as long as requested
Skill finder –Pakaṭai
The ends will win
I will feed the horse
I will put the shield on the donor
I will make the lock
I will make the way".

Six feet tall, with rounded shoulders, straight chest, curled moustache and half a foot long beautiful hair, he lived with a close friend named Kāttappatturai alias Pūlittēvaṉ, the son of Cittiraputrā Tēvar, who was the guardian of the areas under his Zamin.

Pūlittēvaṉ: Origin and Migration

Pūlittēvaṉ's forefathers were the Maṟavars of Koṇṭiyaṅkōṭṭai in the Cētu region. They are natives of Rāmanātapuram district. In the eighteenth century, Rāmanātapuram district was organised as 'Nāṭu' (Country). The ballad records that the people living in Āppanāṭu, Kiḷuvaināṭu, Akappaṉāṭu and Āṉmanāṭu who were living in poverty due to drought migrated from their towns to survive the famine and took refuge in Tirunelvēli regions called Teṉṉāṭu. It is described in the following folk ballad:

Flying white winged ants
In Rāmanātapuram
Thus, was the organisation of the Nāṭu (region)!
Āppanāṭu, Kiḷuvaināṭu
Akappaṉāṭu, Āṉmanāṭu

All the people who used to live in these areas
Unable to satisfy hunger due to severe famine
Abject poverty can barely survive
All the people who have suffered
A lot for the millet porridge,
All the people who left that village
Migrated towards the south Tirunelveli!
They came in a group
As a family."
[*Talit Kataippāṭalkaḷ* (Dalit Folk Ballads, 2010, pp. 31-32)]

Pūlittēvaṉ was born (1714) to Cittiraputrā Tēvar and to Civaññāṉa Nācciyār from Kaṭalāṭi Maṅkaḷam in Rāmātapuram district, one of the descendants of those who migrated from town to town for survival. His original name is Kāttappatturai. This 'Kāttappa Pūlittēvaṉ' is considered to be the tenth in his line of descent. He is also considered as the hero of the freedom struggle (A. Suganthi Annathai, 2019: 191).

In order to confirm that the origin of the Maṟavars, the ancestors of Pūlittēvaṉ, is Rāmātapuram district, it is said that "about 120 chieftains came to the Sethu country and then there were fights among them, and during the conflict, the original Maṟavars migrated and lived along the coast towards Tirunelvēli. They lived from Kaḷakkāṭu to Rājapāḷaiyam" (M. Gnanathai, 2006: 40-41). Also, according to the palm leaf manuscripts submitted by Navanīta Kiriṣṇa Marutappa Tēvar in the Tirunelvēli Civil Court in 1922, it is known that the Maṟavars migrated from the Rāmātapuram area to Ūttumalai in Tirunelvēli region in the eleventh century (S. Sakthivel, 2000: 25). Thurston (2003: 23) says that the Maṟavars were one of the first Dravidian tribes to settle in the south. Fawcett (1993: 57-65) considers Koṇṭaiyaṅkōṭṭai Maṟavars as one of the southern Dravidian tribes.

The interview of former panchayat president Taṉuṣkōṭi Tēvar of Pūlittēvaṉ area on the border of Kaṭalāṭi Maṅkaḷam village in

Rāmātapuram district is to prove that Pūlittēvaṉ and his ancestors were not affected by Cevvayal Pāḷaiyam or Zamin. There was an abject poverty. It was a difficult time for pearl millet porridge and finger millet porridge. The women of Pūlittēvaṉ's ancestral family went to Tirunelvēli to survive the famine without even half a stomach of porridge. One of the women who was pregnant left the town. The woman gives birth to twins in that place. The mother of the twins started working as a labourer in the fields to survive hunger and bring up the children to a zamin belonging to the Pakaṭai clan (Aruntatiyar) who was ruling the Neṟkaṭṭāṉ Cevvayal area [Nakkīraṉ (Tamil magazine) 2002, January, 29]. Taṉuṣkōṭi Tēvar, who belongs to Maṟavar community, is absolutely sure that Pūlittēvaṉ is the descendant of those twins. At the same time, there is evidence that Pūlittēvaṉ's descendants lived as the indigenous people of Āvuṭaiyārpuram, a region near Neṟkaṭṭāṉ Cevvayal. S. Rasu mentions that in one of the Pūlittēvaṉ era copperplates is written, 'Āvuṭaiyārpuram Zamindar Pūlittēvaṉ is our saviour' (A. Suganthi Annathai, 2019: 191).

Neṟkaṭṭāṉ Cevvayal was built by Cakkiliyars, the ancestors of Oṇṭivīraṉ, before the ancestors of Pūlittēvaṉ settled in Cevvayal areas. "In the beginning, Neṟkaṭṭāṉ Cevvayal was a dense forest. The Aruntatiyar (Cakkiliyar, Pakaṭai) tribe cleared the forest and converted it into paddy-growing land." (N. Rasaiah, 2005: 60). This opinion of N. Rasaiah, who has done a historical study of Pūlittēvaṉ, confirms that Cakkilyars are the original inhabitants of Cevvayal and also proves that they are the sons of the soil. In that way, Oṇṭivīraṉ is the only 'son of the soil' of Neṟkaṭṭāṉ Cevvayal, which needs no better proof than this.

Tēvar Clan and their Guardian Deities

During the Pāṇṭiyā rule, the ancestors of Pūlittēvaṉ were appointed as security guards. Among the Tēvar community, men who lived in Āvuṭaiyārpuram, worked as security guards and women worked in the fields for their daily living. In this situation Oṇṭivīraṉ got married to his uncle's daughter Vīrammā. A boy was born to this couple. They were happy to name him 'Kālāṭi'. Unfortunately, Oṇṭivīraṉ's father Pettavīraṉ passes away due to fate. The protector, Oṇṭivīraṉ becomes the leader of Neṟkaṭṭāṉ Cevvayal where his father ruled. His close friend, Pūlittēvaṉ, was guarding the north side of Neṟkaṭṭāṉ Cevvayal area and his father was guarding the west side of the village. As he guarded the north direction, he was called 'Northern Pūlittēvaṉ' by everyone. Oṇṭivīraṉ and Pūlittēvaṉ, who are of similar age and good friends, ruled this region together. The ballad says that both of them ruled like brothers without caste differences and were in harmony and support of each other in administration:

"He became the leader himself
Where his father once ruled
In the future
His close friend Pūlittēvaṉ
Guarded the city
As a supporter of the Protector Oṇṭivīraṉ
Pūlittēvaṉ administered the city
He ruled very well."
[*Talit Kataippāṭalkaḷ* (Dalit Folk Ballads, 2010, p. 37)]

Changes in Pāṇṭiyar -Nāyakkar Rule

During the Pāṇṭiyar rule, Southern Pāṇṭiyar region was divided into 52 administrative blocks. This practice changed during the Nāyakkar rule. That is, Southern Pāṇṭiyar region, which was divided into 52 divisions, was divided into 72 Pāḷaiyams during Nāyakkar reign. There were sixteen Tamil Pāḷaiyams and fifty-six Telugu Pāḷaiyams. Neṟkaṭṭāṉ Cevvayal was the headquarters of all such sixteen Tamil Pāḷaiyams. The rulers of the Pāḷaiyams were called Poligars.

Leadership of Oṇṭivīraṉ in Pāḷaiyam

After Neṟkaṭṭāṉ Cevvayal was converted into Pāḷaiyam, our

Hero, Oṇṭivīraṉ built strong forts and paid taxes regularly to protect the Pāḷaiyam and the people. As 'Northern Pūlittēvaṉ', Pūlittēvaṉ used to guard the northern part of the town. When Arcot was the headquarters of all the Pāḷaiyams, all the Poligars paid tax to the Nawab of Arcot. Oṇṭivīraṉ appointed Iruḷappa Piḷḷai and Pūlittēvaṉ as accountants to pay tax on behalf of Neṟkaṭṭāṉ Cevvayal.

Manipulation and Change of Regime

Due to the manipulations of Iruḷappa Piḷḷai and the incidents of caste abuse in Tamil Nadu, and the increase in population of Tēvar community people, Pūlittēvaṉ wanted to take over the leadership of Pāḷaiyam. Pūlittēvaṉ made friendship artfully with other Pāḷaiyam residents and went to see the Nawab and took the leadership of the Pāḷaiyam in his hands cunningly. The folk ballad records this incident as follows:

"Iruḷappa Piḷḷai and Pūlittēvaṉ
Are those who planned meticulously?
By the urge to conquer
While losing one's virtue
Just listening to the slogan
One who knows how to dissolve stone?
Can dissolve it
To become the leader himself
With such thoughts in mind
He became the ruler
Not only of Tēvar clan
But also gradually of the whole of
Neṟkaṭṭāṉ Cevvayal village"
[*Talit Kataippāṭalkaḷ* (Dalit Folk Ballads, 2010, p. 39-40)]

Considering the future gains, Nawab himself made Pūlittēvaṉ as the Chieftain of Neṟkaṭṭāṉ Cevvayal Pāḷaiyam. The famous

Aruntatiyar Oṇṭivīraṉ Pāḷaiyam turned into Pūlittēvaṉ Pāḷaiyam just like 'an outsider Piṭāri (female village deity with protruding tongue and holding a trident) who wanted a shelter starts chasing away the local Piṭāri who gave her the shelter'. Oṇṭivīraṉ, who gave up the leadership for his close friend Pūlittēvaṉ and for the unity of the country, assumed the responsibility of the army commander. He himself led the war against the enemy. Both the friends ruled Pāḷaiyam together patriotically. In the art of warfare, Oṇṭivīraṉ, who has the ability to act according to the situation, was called with a nickname 'sword' by Pūlittēvaṉ.

Land Rights War

A patriotic hero, he engaged his people, the Aruntatiyars, in the art of war for the sake of the country. It shows the devotion of the hero towards his mother land. On the one hand, they wanted to recognise the leadership of Pūlittēvaṉ and on the other hand Iruḷappa Piḷḷai and the Tēvars took over the lands of Aruntatiyars. Having lost their lands to alcoholism, the Aruntatiyars remained as warriors and were deceived as landless paupers.

The British provided military assistance to the Nawab of Arcot and thereby took charge of tax collection in the Pāḷaiyams. In 1755, Oṇṭivīraṉ and Pūlittēvaṉ objected to the British who went to collect tax by saying why they should pay tax to a foreigner.

"When Heron (British army commander)
Came directly to collect tax
And it was only when the soldier came and asked for tax
In Neṟkaṭṭum Cevvayal
Did Pūlittēvaṉ rise up in rage and said
'It is appropriate to pay taxes
To those who belong to my land'
To a foreigner
Why should we pay tax?
Both the men (Oṇṭivīraṉ and Pūlittēvaṉ)

Began the first battle against the white men", say folk ballads [*Talit Kataippāṭalkaḷ* (Dalit Folk Ballads, 2010, p. 44)]

Pūlittēvaṉ's Disappearance: Myth and Reality

On May 13, 1767, the army under the British commander Donald Campbell attacked Neṟkaṭṭāṉ Cevvayal. Their swords and spears were no match against the powerful cannons of the white man. Knowing well that he could not fight back and should not be trapped by the enemy, Pūlittēvaṉ leaves the fort through the tunnel and escapes to his hometown Kaṭalāṭi. The following ballad thus describes:

"Unable to wage war
Against the enemy
The leader Pūlittēvaṉ
Hurriedly left fort
Through the tunnel
For his hometown Kaṭalāṭi"
[*Talit Kataippāṭalkaḷ* (Dalit Folk Ballads, 2010: 56)].

Then from there he goes to Pāḷaiyamkōṭṭai. Pūlittēvaṉ went to Caṅkaraṉkōvil knowing that Pāḷaiyamkōṭṭai was under British surveillance. He entered Āvuṭaiya Nācciyār temple and disappeared with the plan of escaping from the English soldiers who were encircling him to trap him. All that was left was to wait for the British soldiers who surrounded the temple. Pūlittēvaṉ entered the temple and never came back. When the English soldiers opened their eyes, they saw legs, arms and handcuffs lying there. Pūlittēvaṉ was missing. Those who saw this miracle were stunned. *Pūlittēvaṉ Cintu* mentions about the death of Pūlittēvaṉ that he attained salvation at the feet of Caṅkara Kōmati's sacred fire (Sanmugasundaram, 2007: 591).

"Southern Country Pūlittēvaṉ
Became famous in the temple

Caṅkaraṉ Kōmālayā
Attained salvation at the feet
Of Civaliṅkā.
The Supreme Being has now
Achieved the Sainthood"
(*Pūlittēvaṉ Cintu* - 591).

This being the case, it is noteworthy that the Collector of Tirunelvēli mentioned in his letter (12.9.1836) that Pūlittēvaṉ was arrested in 1767 and died in 1768 in Pāḷaiyamkōṭṭai Jail. However, the true picture of Pūlittēvaṉ's death (1767) remains a mystery as there is no definite information about Pūlittēvaṉ's death. Born in a valiant Maṟavar clan, he was pious, did involve in many charities, did undertake many temple renovations, was not a coward, and above all fought the first war against the whites for the freedom of India; the death of Pūlittēvaṉ from South India is not a natural death but still remains a mystery.

This eighteenth century event is neither realistic nor rational in today's life. Rather it seems to be a myth. This because the mythology and Bhakti literary texts tell us that eighth century Tiruppāṇāḻvār, ninth century Āṇṭāḷ, Vaḷḷalār merged with 'Jōti' (sacred fire), Nantaṉ merged with god. In the history of Bhakti literature, while this fictional legend is subject to doubt and reconsideration, it appears to be a fabricated story that Pūlittēvaṉ, who lived in the eighteenth century AD, united with 'Jōti' (sacred fire) or merged with the lord Civā. This may be an attempt to augment him into godly status. In other words people tried to deify Pūlittēvaṉ. So, in the eyes of historians, the disappearance of Pūlittēvaṉ is presumed to be mysterious.

Neṟkaṭṭāṉ Cevvayal's Present Status

Ezhil Ilangovaṉ (2010:33) mentions that after Pūlittēvaṉ's death, Oṇṭivīraṉ again took charge of the Palayam and Pūlittēvaṉ's sons Civañāṉa Pāṇṭiyaṉ, Cittiraputrā Tēvar and daughter Kōmati Muttu Talaicci under his protection for four years. The following dalit folk ballad depicts how after the death of Pūlittēvaṉ, Oṇṭivīraṉ took over the leadership of the Pāḷaiyam.

"After the death of Pūlittēvaṉ
A famous warrior
Of Neṟkaṭṭāṉ Cevvayal Pāḷaiyam
He directly took responsibility
As a chief of Pāḷaiyam
The Pakaṭai leader took charge"
[*Talit Kataippāṭalkaḷ* (Dalit Folk Ballads, 2010: 57)]

Subsequently, in the battles of Kaḷakkāṭu, Kaṅkaikoṇṭāṉ, Tiruvillipputtūr and Putukkōṭṭai, he became a threat to the British government and won the battle. The great warrior Oṇṭivīraṉ died on the battlefield in the final 'Battle of Tēṉmalai'. Oṇṭivīraṉ has the honour of being the first king (1771) who fought against the British and died on the battlefield. His death is described in the following lines:

"He fought the war valiantly
By the help of the allied forces
And its gunfire
He died a heroic death!"
[*Talit Kataippāṭalkaḷ* (Dalit Folk Ballads, 2010: 57)]

After the death of Oṇṭivīraṉ, the Tēvar community people who settled from many villages became the majority of Neṟkaṭṭāṉ Cevvayal, and the native people Aruntatiyars became a minority and landless due to the large number of deaths in the battlefield. The dalit folk ballads stand testimony to this fact.

"After the death of Oṇṭivīraṉ
Thevar community people
Got together and
Gave caste as an excuse
Chased away all the Cakkiliyars

And sent them to
The Eastern part of the village"
[*Talit Kataippāṭalkaḷ* (Dalit Folk Ballads, 2010: 59)]

After their lands were confiscated and their possessions lost, they migrated to Muṉār, Kōvilpaṭṭi, Tūttukkuṭi, Tirunelvēli, Caṅkaraṉkōvil and teṉkāci to survive the famine. The rest of the original natives were resettled in a place called 'Paccēri' in the eastern part of Neṟkaṭṭāṉ Cevvayal.

Oṇṭivīraṉ is still worshipped by the people of Kaṭalāṭi, the native place of Pūlittēvaṉ.

"The great warrior Oṇṭivīraṉ
Although disappeared from the village
His legacy still lives
In people's minds
He is worshipped
As a deity
By the people of Tēvar community
At Kaṭalāṭi"
[*Talit Kataippāṭalkaḷ* (Dalit Folk Ballads, 2010: 60)]

Aruntatiyars worship Oṇṭivīraṉ as their family deity and as a cult in Pacuvantaṉai, Kuruvikuḷam and Paruttikkuḷam. After Pūlittēvaṉ's death in 1767, Oṇṭivīraṉ protected his people and family for a period of four years. As a mark of love and respect for him, the Tēvar community still worships Oṇṭivīraṉ as a guardian deity.

Revolutionary Salute to Oṇṭivīraṉ

After the death of Oṇṭivīraṉ, his descendants, those who marvelled at his bravery, those who participated in the liberation war against the whites, those who believed in his good conduct, those who benefited from him, those who were protected by him, and those who respected him, are paying homage and tribute to

Oṇṭivīraṉ. Children born in their families are named 'Oṇṭivīraṉ' and 'Vīraṉ' in honour of Oṇṭivīraṉ. People are worshipping Oṇṭivīraṉ as the main deity and sub-deity in some villages in southern districts. 'Sri Oṇṭivīraṉcāmi Temple' is located in the village of Āttaṅkarai in Viḷāttikuḷam area of Tūttukkuṭi district. The people of Tēvar community in this area are worshipping this Oṇṭivīraṉ as their god. The poet Pāskaratās recorded in his diary (29.10.1939 - Nākalāpuram) that he had gone to this Āttaṅkarai Oṇṭivīraṉ temple with his children. Various communities living in Sivakasi and its surrounding areas of Tamil Nadu are worshipping Oṇṭivīraṉ as a sub-deity in their ancestral temples. But there is no evidence that Pūlittēvaṉ is worshiped by Aruntatiyars in any village of Tamil Nadu.

Basic Facts as stated by the Sources

Based on the available sources that Pūlittēvaṉ's ancestors used to work as guards and labourers in Neṟkaṭṭāṉ Cevvayal areas, based on the opinions of scholars like Rācaiyā, Thurston, Sakthivel, etc., and based on Taṉuṣkōṭi Tēvar's interview and Oṇṭivīraṉ folk ballads, some basic facts are clearly established. They are as follows:

1. The people of Aruntatiyar have had a glorious past and a long history of their own. It is deliberately unwritten/unrecorded and hidden.

2. Oṇṭivīraṉ's ancestors were the actual landholders of the Neṟkaṭṭāṉ Cevvayal area and Oṇṭivīraṉ was the chief of the same Palayam at some point in time.

3. In the seventeenth and eighteenth centuries, Aruntatiyars were small and large landowners, peasants and zamindars in some parts of Tamil Nadu.

4. Pūlittēvaṉ and his ancestors were in no way entitled to the Neṟkaṭṭāṉ Cevvayal Pāḷaiyam or the Zamin.

5. Pūlittēvaṉ's ancestors were the planners of Āvuṭaiyārpuram (Putukkōṭṭai) area.

6. Pūlittēvaṉ was originally from Rāmanātapuram; his hometown was Mangalam near Kaṭalāṭi.
7. The people of Tirunelvēli who cleared and reformed the dense forest area and created Neṟkaṭṭāṉ Cevvayal were the Cakkiliyars of Tirunelvēli.
8. The Cakkiliyars ruled Neṟkaṭṭāṉ Cevvayal and Pāpanācam hill regions.
9. Although the ancestors of Pūlittēvaṉ lived in fortified palaces, they worked as security guards for the Poligars/ Zamindars.
10. There were twin Pāḷaiyams of Neṟkaṭṭāṉ Cevvayal – Āvuṭaiyārpuram.
11. Pūlittēvaṉ must have captured Neṟkaṭṭāṉ Cevvayal and shifted his headquarters from Āvuṭaiyārpuram to Neṟkaṭṭāṉ Cevvayal.
12. After Pūlittēvaṉ's death, Oṇṭivīraṉ again took charge of the Pāḷaiyam and kept Pūlittēvaṉ's heirs under his protection for four years.
13. Oṇṭivīraṉ is worshipped as a deity by the Tēvars in Kaṭalāṭi, the native place of Pūlittēvaṉ.
14. There is no evidence that Pūlittēvaṉ is worshipped by Aruntatiyars in any village in Tamil Nadu.
15. On the whole, the fact that the historians have recorded Neṟkaṭṭāṉ Cevvayal Pāḷaiyam as Pūlittēvaṉ's Pāḷaiyam is an unhistorical and aberrant news. Oṇṭivīraṉ's ancestors were the original landowners of Cevvayal Pāḷaiyam area in Tirunelvēli district.

Chapter - 6

Oṇṭivīraṉ in Tamil Society

Oṇṭivīraṉ's ancestors were the original landowners of Neṟkaṭṭāṉ Cevvayal Pāḷaiyam area in Tirunelvēli district. "Neṟkaṭṭāṉ Cevvayal Zameen, the Aruntatiyars who lived in the land surrounding it, were the landowners of that time". This is proved by Ezhil Ilangovan's comment that these include small and large landowners.

True history has been distorted due to the fact that there are no inscriptions, copperplates, literature, or documents written on palm leaves among the illiterate Aruntatiyar people. We have already seen the history of Oṇṭivīraṉ, who is said to be the army general of Pūlittēvaṉ. This chapter aims to introduce some other heroic personalities who lived and died in the Tamil community with the same name.

Kuruvikuḷam Oṇṭivīraṉ

Popular narratives say that a person named Oṇṭivīraṉ lived in Kuruvikuḷam, Tirunelvēli district. He was killed by the dominant caste and deified. Kuruvikuḷam, a town in Caṅkaraṉkōvil taluka, is also the headquarters of the panchayat union with the same name. Oṇṭivīraṉ was one of those who used to work as a guard for a Zamindar from Telugu-speaking Nāyakkar community in this village. Belonging to the Aruntatiyar community, he had the prowess to tame bulls. Attracted by his bravery and beauty, a Nāyakkar community girl called Erram'māḷ who lived in this town, fell in love with him. The love between the two became known to many. The people of Nāyakkar community, who could not bear the love of young Cakkiliyar man, got annoyed with him.

The Nāyakkar community, unwilling to confront him directly as he was a warrior and a palace guard, decided to kill him by trickery. Accordingly, they brought a bull in drunken state and asked Oṇṭivīraṉ to tame it. Unaware that the bull was intoxicated, Oṇṭivīraṉ approached the bull and it pounced on Oṇṭivīraṉ and ran away carrying his body on its horns. Even after the death of Oṇṭivīraṉ, who was pierced by a horn, the bull ran carrying his corpse. After a long journey, the Aruntatiyars took the body of Oṇṭivīraṉ, who slipped down from the horn, and burnt it. Aruntatiyars used to worship the place where both of them were cremated. Later, idols are made for both of them and they were worshipped. There is also a custom of naming a male child as Oṇṭivīraṉ and a female child as Erram'māḷ (A. Sivasubramanian, 2010: 31-32).

Cūrappaṭṭu Oṇṭivīraṉ

Oṇṭivīraṉ temple is located in the village of Cūrappaṭṭu on the highway from Ampattūr to Puḻal near Chennai. The groom of this village is Oṇṭivīraṉ. His native village and name are not known. Many years ago he married a girl in this village. He is very strong. Proficient in many heroic sports like Cilampam (a weapon-based Indian martial art from Tamil Nadu), Kabaddi and Wrestling. Oṇṭivīraṉ, who was a drunkard, used to cause a lot of trouble to the people like fighting with the people of the neighbouring villages after drinking alcohol, robbing the passers-by, robbing the goats, cows and grains from the stores at night. Due to him, the surrounding villages were facing many hardships and sufferings.

His brothers-in-law lost patience as they received many complaints against him and wondered what to do with him. They asked Oṇṭivīraṉ's wife for her opinion. She too, in her unquenchable anger against Oṇṭivīraṉ, took the opportunity to kill him and the Cūrappaṭṭu brothers and the conspirators planned to kill Oṇṭivīrann. They were afraid to fight face to face with the mighty Oṇṭivīraṉ. They tried to solve it in a deceitful way. One evening they made Oṇṭivīraṉ drink too much alcohol and staggered and hacked him to pieces.

From the day of Oṇṭivīraṉ's death, animals in Cūrappaṭṭu village, suddenly fell to their deaths. A severe fever spread among the people. No woman in the village could give birth to any children. Even if pregnant women from other places come to this place, their embryos got aborted. As the situation persisted for several months, the people of the village got together and called a preacher to perform puja (religious rites). The preacher went on to say that Oṇṭivīraṉ was the cause of all the bad omens happening in the village. The next day, Oṇṭivīraṉ appeared in the dreams of the villagers and disappeared saying that if they built a 'Pīṭam' (a kind of pedestal or a raised platform built of stone) and worshipped him, he would protect everyone and give them the boons they asked for.

Since then, the people of Cūrappaṭṭu have been gathering together, erecting a pedestal and worshipping Oṇṭivīraṉ. They happily named their first male child as Oṇṭivīraṉ. Oṇṭivīraṉ also fulfils the demands of all the people, not only the people of the village, but also the people from outside the villages and the passers-by, and has been protecting them. It is said that Cūrappaṭṭu Oṇṭivīraṉ belonged to the Vaṉṉiyar community. Oṇṭivīraṉ is worshipped by the Vaṉṉiyar and Reṭṭiyār communities and also by the motorists on the highway from Ampattūr to Puḻal. In this temple there is a horse as the vehicle of Oṇṭivīraṉ. A special pooja is held at the Oṇṭivīraṉ temple on all Wednesdays (Informant: Oṇṭivīraṉ Temple Priest, Age : 80, Community : Vaṉṉiyar, Place: Cūrappaṭṭu).

Kaṭalāṭi Maṅkaḷam: Noṇṭivīraṉ (a Hero with a broken leg)

This heroic person belongs to the Aruntatiyar caste of Kaṭalāṭi Maṅkaḷam village in Rāmanātapuram district. Pūlittēvaṉ is a native of this village. Pūlittēvaṉ, who was the commander of Neṟkaṭṭāṉ Cevvayal Pāḷaiyam, was suffering from insufficient force when he decided to fight against the Whites. Through his grandmothers he came to know the origin of Maṅkaḷam village, the native village. Pūlittēvaṉ left for his native village Maṅkaḷam after evading the Whites by building an underground tunnel in the Caṅkaraṉkōvil and leading a life of hiding. He said to his countrymen, 'Are you coming with me to fight against the Whites?'

As soon as he heard this, Oṇṭivīraṉ belonging to the Aruntatiyar class of Maṅkaḷam village with two thousand foot soldiers and a Veṇṇimalai alias Veṇṇikkālāṭi with two thousand cavalry soldiers set out with Pūlittēvaṉ in battle towards Neṟkaṭṭāṉ Cevvayal. Oṇṭivīraṉ and Veṇṇimalai met the expectations of Pūlittēvaṉ and fought with the whites in the battle that took place at a rapid pace, and the white army was scattered on all four sides. Pūlittēvaṉ appointed Oṇṭivīraṉ and Veṇṇimalai as his chief commanders. Realising that these warlike men were so 'invincible', the Britishers launched a heavy attack with modern guns and artillery in the next phase of the war. The Pūlittēvaṉ force suffered heavy losses in this battle. Oṇṭivīraṉ, one of the chief commanders, loses his leg in the battle, and Oṇṭivīraṉ returns to his hometown Maṅkaḷam with a broken leg.

Since the Oṇṭivīraṉ who went to war as a hero came back with a broken leg, the hero was called 'Noṇṭivīraṉ' (Heroic warrior with a broken leg). The Tēvars of Maṅkaḷam village is worshipping Oṇṭivīraṉ of Aruntatiyar clan, who went to fight for the country of his birth without expecting any recompense. Later they built a temple for the crippled man and have been worshipping him as their 'Kulacāmi' (deity worshipped by generations in a clan). The people of Maṅkaḷam village take pride in worshipping Noṇṭivīraṉ, a member of the Aruntatiyar caste, as a Kulacāmi. From that time till now, the entire people of Maṅkaḷam village go to Noṇṭivīraṉ temple to pray and the people of the village still have the belief that they will get the desired result. The people of our village still believe that 'whether it is going out for a hunt, contesting an election, or going to a lawsuit, if you go to Noṇṭivīraṉ temple and light camphor, take soil and apply it on your forehead, victory is guaranteed'. Ravināyakam, a young graduate of the village who says that Noṇṭivīraṉ who has become a god is a 'guardian deity' for us, says with great confidence. He also goes on to say, 'What is the relationship between god and caste?' [Kishore, *Nakkīraṉ* (Tamil Magazine): 29.01.2002].

Oṇṭivīraṉ in Noṇṭi Nāṭakam (a play on Oṇṭivīraṉ)

In 1886, a Tamil poet Muttālaṅkuṟicci Kantacāmi wrote a seminal book titled *Tiruccentūr Noṇṭi Nāṭakam.* This book is completely different from other 'plays on lame people'. As the author has mentioned 'Tiruccentūr' (Tiruccentūr, which is hailed as the second house of Lord Murugan) in the title of this book, there is room to assume that this is a book about the Tamil deity Murugan. But if we analyse this play, it is revealed that Tiruccentūr has introduced the history of 'Noṇṭivīraṉ' into the story in the process of singing the praises of Lord Murugan and written the play. But, other programmatic elements of this book, including the worship of God, focus on the life of Oṇṭivīraṉ, the leader and commander of Neṟkaṭṭāṉ Cevvayal Pāḷaiyam.

In the story of this book, the protagonist's desire to see the South, getting caught in the trap of Citamparam Tāci (Citamparam temple danseuses), escaping to Tañcāvūr after seeing the siege, stealing a horse from Tirukkāṭṭuppaḷḷi, entering Pāḷaiyam in disguise, befriending the people of Turaicāni, training in horse training, entering stable to steal a horse, hiding in a closet/pothole, encircling by Turaicāni and Paṟaiyar, surrendering to the security chief, struggling with no way to escape, trapping byToṇṭaimāṉ, ridiculing by the villagers, leading to the battleground, losing of arm, leg as punishment, supporting Vaḷḷal[1]Aṉanta Patmanāpaṉ, leaving Tirukkāṭṭuppaḷḷi and reaching Tiruccentūr, seeing Lord Senthil and worshipping Lord Murugan in a dream, removing sins and growing hands and feet. Therefore, looking at the elements

1. The one who gives the things without saying no to those who ask.

of achieving well-being, it seems that the poet Kantacāmi must have written the book *Tiruccentūr Noṇṭi Nāṭakam* with the life of Oṇṭivīraṉ as its theme. "If we carefully look at the elements of the story used by the poet Kantacāmi in his play *Tiruccentūr Noṇṭi Nāṭakam*, it is clear that he has created the character of Noṇṭivīraṉ with the character of Oṇṭivīraṉ in mind", says the historian Rasaiah (1990 :15).

Poet Kandasamy should have written the book *Tiruccentūr Noṇṭi Nāṭakam* to make the people of Tamil Nadu aware of the freedom spirit against the British. His patriotism and courage are shown by his attempt to write this book at the height of Britishers' oppression. In that way, there is a place to consider the book *Tiruccentūr Noṇṭi Nāṭakam* as a clear lifetime experience of the poet Kantacāmi on the feeling of freedom struggle.

Oṇṭivīraṉs - Political Rights

Lately, Needhicharan, the founder and president of the Indian Ganasangam, has been claiming that "Nāmakkal is the birthplace of Oṇṭivīraṉ". People of this region claim that Oṇṭivīraṉ's native place is Kaṇappilpāḷaiyam which is located in Elaccipāḷaiyam in Iluppuli village, Nāmakkal district and more than four thousand relatives of Oṇṭivīraṉ's Maṅkavāṟu clan worship Oṇṭivīraṉ as their family deity. They claim that they separated from Kaṇappilpāḷaiyam and built a separate temple and that there is a 250-year-old neem tree with five branches at the place where Oṇṭivīraṉ died, and that the temple has been under the control of the Hindu Charities Department since 1924. The people of Southern district of Tamil Nadu strongly that Nāmakkal has nothing to do with Oṇṭivīraṉ and that it is highly condemnable. Needhicharan's lobbying appears to be claiming the fame of Oṇṭivīraṉ by presenting artificial reasons in a bid to appropriate the history. This shows Needhicharan's ignorance and misunderstanding and of Oṇṭivīraṉ's history.

R. Murugesan Pagadai, who claims to be the seventh generation heir of Oṇṭivīraṉ, claims that Oṇṭivīraṉ belonged to Caṅkakiri area. In a letter written to Nāmakkal Aruntatiyar Kāṇcaṅkām, he presents, thus, his claim. That is, 'Oṇṭivīraṉ worked as a guard and commander in Caṅkakiri Orukkamālai Pāḷaiyam in 1755. While working here, he fell in love with a young girl named Nallam'māḷ from the Vēṭṭuvakulam community who was selling curd in the area. Nallam'māḷ's relatives came to know about their close relationship and strongly opposed Oṇṭivīraṉ. At the end there was a fierce fight. In this fight, many members of Vēṭṭuvakulam community are killed. Oṇṭivīraṉ, who escaped from this, joins Pūlittēvaṉ's army at Tirunelveli. Then Oṇṭivīraṉ fought against the whites in Neṟkaṭṭāṉ Cevvayal and won the war. Then he came back from Tirunelvēli to his hometown Nāmakkal Kaṇappilpāḷaiyam and died a heroic death on 20th August 1772 AD. At the same place, the heirs of Oṇṭivīraṉ and the members of the Maṅkavāṟu clan celebrate a temple festival for three days in the full moon of the month of February every five years, says R. Murugesan Pagadai.

In Indian freedom struggle historical documents and oral histories, we find Oṇṭivīraṉ's clan name as Pakaṭai only. Nowhere does the clan name 'Maṅkavāṟu' claimed by Needhicharan appear after Oṇṭivīraṉ's name. K. Jakkaiyyan records that the era of Oṇṭivīraṉ ended with the Battle of Tēṉmalai, when Oṇṭivīraṉ destroyed the enemy's camp and remained a nightmare for the enemy until 1771, even after the death of Pūlittēvaṉ in 1767. So, it seems clear that Oṇṭivīraṉ who participated in the Indian Freedom Struggle is different from the Oṇṭivīraṉ claimed by Needhicharan and R. Murugesan Pagadai.

Chapter - 7

Unknown Aruntatiyar Clans

From Nature Worship to Tribal Deity Worship

'Do not live in a town which doesn't have a temple' is the belief of Tamils. In primitive times, man depended on nature and later lived on it. He started worshipping nature as a result of the benefits resulting from his faith in nature. Man's spirit worship began with the death of his ancestors. Then he started worshipping animals and birds as their clan/tribal symbols. He continued to worship objects with supernatural powers, believing them to have supernatural powers. Then he started worshipping the ancestors by putting a stone for the dead. Ancestor worship continued as family members worshipping ancestors who had died of natural causes. Ancestor worship eventually became Clan Deity Worship.

Clan deity worship is a component of deity worships. Most of the people of Tamil Nadu are worshipping minor deities, but due to various social, economic, political and cultural reasons, worshipping the dead person (death due to suicide, war, murder, accident etc.) as a deity is called tribal or clan deity worship (Marc, 2001: 91).

S. Sakthivel, a folklorist, presents the following as symbols and forms of worship of minor deities. They are: Minor deities who have birth and death and have specific powers. Temples with minor deities often have non-Brahmins as priests. In these temples, where only the people who don't have enough education or training to understand something in detail can worship, there is definitely a sacrifice. There is no distinction between Cāyvā and Vaiṣṇavā among minor deities. Non-vegetarian substances are used for offerings. Idols are created by people and maintained by people. The idols enshrined in roofs, stone, wood and hood have a monstrous form. Minor deities are considered to live in this world. It is based on Little Tradition and related to village life (Marc, 2007: 325-327).

Types of Folk Deities

S. Sakthivel divides folk deities into five categories as: 1. Male deities, 2. Female deities, 3. Caste deities, 4. Camāti deities (those who have died while meditating), 5. Mālai deities (those who have attained the status of god by diving into fire). Among these Jakkam'mātēvi, Pom'māttā (Kampaḷattu Nāyakkar), Cauṭam'māḷ (Tēvāṅkar), Vaṇṭumalaiyāṉ (Ceṅkunta Mutaliyār) and Pattirakāḷi (Nāṭār) are defined as caste deities. These caste deities are often popularly known in their respective localities and are recorded in inscriptions.

This chapter records the history of the two clan deities involved in the murder of Cērvāraṉ Cāmi and Muttuvīraṉ Cāmi, the influential clan members of the Aruntatiyar people of Tamil Nadu.

Cērvāraṉ Cāmi, Muttuvīraṉ Cāmi - Clan Deities who rose due to their untimely murder

The caste problem that continues today dates back to centuries. Upper castes, middle castes, and lower castes fall into three groups, and if they fall in love with each other and marry each other, they will forgive and tolerate it without taking it to the point of murder. But many Tamil stories tell that if a love marriage takes place between the upper caste, lower caste, or middle caste, it often ends in murder as a caste conflict. It is defined as 'honour killing' which takes place on the basis of caste. Such murders are happening all over the country. That is how the murders of

Cērvāraṉ and Muttuvīraṉ of Aruntatiyar clan took place. The unknown history of honour killing of Cērvāraṉ and Muttuvīraṉ gathered through field research has come to light.

Cērvāraṉ was born into a low caste Cakkiliyar clan. His girlfriend belonged to the Veḷḷāḷar caste, a middle caste. The love between them forces them to leave the town at a certain time. As a result they leave the town and get married without anyone noticing. Knowing this, the girl's own brothers who belong to the Vellalar caste chase them away and kill them. In this fight Cērvāraṉ kills all his attackers. The dead lovers Cērvāraṉ and Kāmāṭci went to Kailācam[1] and received boons from Lord Sivā and then came to the earth and established themselves as deities and showered blessings on the people. Their history is vividly told in the following Cērvāraṉ Cāmi story.

Cērvāraṉ Cāmi - History, Worship and Rituals

There was a man from Aruntatiyar caste lived in Northern Tamil country called Cērvāraṉ. He is called Cakkliyan and Mātiyaṉ by his caste name. He was a cobbler and looked very handsome and fit. That is to say, he was seven feet tall with a fair complexion, a knife-like moustache, a turban tied on his head. He was so attractive that no woman would ever miss to look at him. One day as he was passing through the street, Kāmāṭci, who was on top of the mansion, fell in love with his charm and elegance. Enchanted by his beauty, she decided to marry him and make him as her husband.

To fulfil her wish, she called her seven brothers and asked them to sew her nice pair of sandals. Accepting the request of the lovely sister, the brothers invited the shoemaker there. Cērvāraṉ who came to the mansion measured Kāmāṭci's feet and made her a pair of beautiful and suitable sandals. Cērvāraṉ, who came to Kāmāṭci's house thinking that he could go and get a wage after giving away the sandal, waited for their brothers. He called her brothers but her brothers were not present in Kāmāṭci's house

1. Kailācam is a famous mountain in the Kailai range of the Himalayas.

at that time. In response, she raised her voice from inside and said, "Bring them to the front house and I should not come out." Hearing this, Cērvāraṉ went to the front house as she called, and Kāmāṭci called him into the next inner room. After entering the house, both these lovers were mesmerised by the beauty and stood staring at each other. This meeting blossomed into love between them. Lovers who liked each other planned to hold hands later.

Realising that marrying against her brothers' opposition was impossible and therefore Kāmāṭci decided to leave her parents and brothers with the goal of living with Cērvāraṉ. United in mind, the two wanted to live together. They also planned to migrate from Northern Tamil Nadu to Southern Tamil Nadu. One day, they left the town without anyone knowing about it. On the way, both of them got married at Vaṇakāḷiyammaṉ shrine. This is how the following lines narrate the incident:

"They also walked
When passing by
The Vaṇakāḷi temple
They got married"

[Cērvāraṉ Cāmi: Varalāṟum Kataippāṭalkaḷum (Cērvāraṉ Cāmi: History and Folk Ballads, 2016, pp. 19: 215 - 219)].

From there they went to a hill in the town of Paṭṭāṭaikaṭṭi, west of Vēlāyutapuram, which is south of Caṅkaraṉkōvil in Tirunelveli district.

Cērvāraṉ and Kāmāṭci had also brought a dog with them. They could not go into the town and live with Aruntatiyar. It is okay if you're an Aruntatiyar woman. How can this village accommodate a rich and beautiful Kāmāṭci from a different caste? Assuming that if they were to live like that, everyone would come and talk to each other and there would be a lot of sensation and unrest, so the two of them built a loft on a hill in the forest in the east of the village and lived there. Cērvāraṉ was living with his wife Kāmāṭci in hiding, hoping that someone would find out if he was within the town limit. He would come down the hill when there was no one, and collect vegetables and other essential products in the forest gardens. When he wandered there for water, he saw a mountain stream, and knowing where it would go, he went there and found a water barge called Paṭṭāṭaikaṭṭi. Every day around 12 noon, when there is no one on the streets, he comes there and takes a bath and goes home with the water he needs. After some time had passed like this, the seven brothers of Kāmāṭci wandered in search of them and came near where they were living. When they came to the pond to water the horses, they asked the shepherd boys about the identity of Cērvāraṉ and Kāmāṭci. After learning the identity of Cērvāraṉ, her brothers asked the children over there. The children said that he wouldn't talk to anyone. They said that he would come here and take a bath and take water. The seven brothers of Kāmāṭci, who immediately planned to capture Cērvāraṉ, tied their horses to hideouts, stayed there for the night, and waited for Cērvāraṉ's arrival until twelve o'clock the next day, armed with swords and knives.

The next day it was twelve o'clock. When Cērvāraṉ came to the water tank as usual and returned after taking a bath, Kāmāṭci's seven brothers came and blocked the way. When Cērvāraṉ did not expect this to happen, one of the brothers cut Cērvāraṉ's stomach with a sword. Immediately, Cērvāraṉ, untying his turban and tying his severed stomach tightly, ran towards the hill where his wife, Kāmāṭci, was standing. The following folk song describes thus,

"The seven people who were hiding in the forest got up
Cērvāraṉ was surrounded
The seven brothers surrounded him when he was not expecting
What to do
At a time when Cērvāraṉ's mind was disturbed
He was surrounded by a crowd
He was attacked and
His stomach was cut

After having received the blow

He untied his turban to wrap the wound

Ran towards his wife in the hill"

[Cērvāraṉ Cāmi: Varalāṟum Kataippāṭalkaḷum (Cērvāraṉ Cāmi: History and Folk Ballads, 2016, pp. 25 - 26, 410 - 423)]

The dog, which was watching it, ran in front of the Cērvāraṉ and grabbed Kāmāṭci's saree. Seeing her seven-foot-tall husband running towards her with a scythe on his stomach, Kāmāṭci ran towards him. Seeing her husband who had run away without counterattacking because they were her brothers, she said, "Don't let them go, even if it's my brothers, kill them." Cērvāraṉ took his wife's word and took it as a boon, chased them away and cut down all the seven brothers. Seeing that Cērvāraṉ, who was hugging his wife Kāmāṭci to his chest, was bleeding due to a cut in his stomach, Kāmāṭci decided that her husband should not die before her, but she should die before him. So, she bit out her tongue and died as a Cumaṅkali (a term used to refer to a married woman who wears the sacred thread tied around her neck by her husband to signify that he is still alive, from the moment it is tied until death, and continues to live with him). Cērvāraṉ also later died. This is described in the following folk ballad on Cērvāraṉ Cāmi.

"When she got to know

That Cērvāraṉ was losing his pulse

And dying

She thought of taking her life

By biting out her tongue

As it is the custom and tradition

That a married woman would

Always prefer to die as Cumaṅkali"

[Cērvāraṉ Cāmi: Varalāṟum Kataippāṭalkaḷum (Cērvāraṉ Cāmi: History and Folk Ballads, 2016, pp. 27: 454 - 465)]

A dog that had been roaming around for two days died there because of the affection shown by its masters. Together with Kāmāṭci's brothers, two of them and nine others lay dead in the forest. Cērvāraṉ and his wife Kāmāṭci evaporated and went to Kailasam (a holy place for Hindus). Knowing the details, Lord Civā gave them a suitable boon and gave them the boon to receive prayers and establish themselves in the world. Accordingly, both of them came into the forest as deities and established themselves.

Cērvāraṉ - A Vibrant Clan Deity

Zamin of Naṭuvakkuṟicci of Tirunelvēli district used to come early every morning on horseback with his troop and taking a bath before sunrise. One such day he came to bathe. After bathing, he got on his horse and when he was riding the horse, the horse collapsed on its leg. Zamin fell down from the horse. Zamin who managed to recover thought that he had fallen down by some mistake and once again mounted the horse and tried to ride again his horse. Even then the horse fell down and so did Zamin, after which Zamin went home on foot. He came to bathe there the next day as well. On returning home, the same thing happened on the first day. Immediately the Zamin summoned the palace astrologer and asked for details. The astrologer, who knew the planetary positions, said that there is a deity stationed at that place, and if you bring it and worship it, your clan will prosper. Immediately they called the neighbouring Zamins like Cokkampaṭṭi Zamin, V.K. Putūr Zamin, Ūttumalai Zamin and other eight Maṟavar Zamins and performed all kinds of rituals with drums and worshipped at the same place. At that time, the grace of the deity did not come to anyone, so no one became frenzy and did not dance by the grace of God. From the next day and for seven days, all the other castes, except the Cakkiliyars, performed puja with a drum and made offerings to Cērvāraṉ Cāmi. Even then none could get trance.

But on the same day when the zamindar asked the astrologer to see the details, the astrologer knew that a Cakkiliyan Cāmi named Cērvāraṉ, standing here as a deity, would come and bless him and give him a blessing. The Astrologer did not share that information with anyone thinking that if he should accept it. On the eighth day, the eight Zamins together summoned the Cakkiliyars and made the offerings to them by beating the drums. Seeing that some of them got trance, the astrologer immediately trampled the stone lying under his feet with his big toe and chanted a mantra to subdue the effect of trance. On that day too everyone returned home disappointed.

When astrologer went home happily and haughtily who had achieved what he had set out to do, all the three hundred cows in his stable died. The astrologer went to call the Cakkiliyaṉ who had been graced by God to take them away as per social custom. When he was told to dispose of the dead cattle, he said, "open our clan deity hidden under the log, I will dispose of the cattle. Realising the mistake, astrologer immediately went and freed Sami, who had been restrained by the mantra, and apologised to Zamin and told the truth.

On hearing what the astrologer said, the Zamin again asked all the zamindars to bow down to the Cakkiliyars by praying to them. Together with the eighteen Cakkiliyar villages of the eight Zamins, they built a temple at the place where Cērvāraṉ was killed and worshipped Cērvāraṉ - Kāmāṭci along with the dog. This is described in the folk ballad as follows:

"For the dog

The next worshipper!

Eighteen Cakkiliyar villages

Together they will worship!

Like this

For everyone

Cērvāraṉ became a deity."

[Cērvāraṉ Cāmi: Varalāṟum Kataippāṭalkaḷum (Cērvāraṉ Cāmi: History and Folk Ballads, 2016, pp. 34 : 685 - 690)]

In front of the temple erected in Paṭṭāṭaikaṭṭi, the place where Cērvāraṉ was killed, the images of the seven brothers of Kāmāṭci are also installed as 'Pūṭams' (a mound built for the little angel to live in). Every year in the month of February during Shivratri festival, the story of Cērvāraṉ - Kāmāṭci is sung from the morning till the dawn of the next day. On those days a man and a woman act out biographical events of Cērvāraṉ - Kāmāṭci by dancing with drums. This event has been held by the Cakkiliyars for many generations at the place where Cērvāraṉ was killed.

Taking soil from the temple built at the place where Cērvāraṉ was killed, the Cakkiliyars of the Southern district of Tamil Nadu have erected a mound in their villages and worshipped every year in the months of February or March. The family deity named Cērvāraṉ has been transformed into a god of worship at the place of murder and due to its influence it has become the people's god in many towns.

The older generation Cakkiliyars used to name one of the male children born in their family as Cērvāraṉ. With the passage of time, this practice has disappeared among the present generation, but they have started naming names starting with the first letter of the name Cērvāraṉ. However, every year they continue to worship Cērvāraṉ Cāmi by making offerings. The belief that 'Cērvāraṉ is a vibrant deity' is still prevalent among other castes including dominant castes of Southern district of Tamil Nadu.

Muttuvīraṉ Cāmi - History and Worship

No written information or stories about Muttuvīraṉ Cāmi are available. However, the history of Muttuvīraṉ Cāmi has been created through the oral stories narrated by Muttam'mā from Tōṇukāl village near Kōvilpaṭṭi. Muttuvīraṉ, a youth belonging to the Aruntatiyar caste, used to work in the houses of dominant caste Thevar in the surrounding areas of Tōṇukāl near Kōvilpaṭṭi. He fell in love with a woman belonging to the Pillai caste. Both of them ran away from the town and lived hidden in the forest area near Tōṇukāl village. The woman's seven brothers, who were looking for the two who had run away, reached the foot of the forest. The dog brought by the brothers surrounded the lovers. When both of them ran away from the dog, they could not make it past the end of the road. Unable to run, Muttuvīraṉ's neck was cut into pieces by his girlfriend's brothers. There is a well to the westside of the village where Muttuvīraṉ was cut into pieces. Muttuvīraṉ's girlfriend was killed by her brothers in the nearby pool. Thus, both became gods.

At the place where Muttuvīraṉ's head was cut off, Muttuvīraṉ Cāmi's statue is erected and Aruntatiyars are still worshipping it. The deceased lover of Muttuvīraṉ is worshipped as a goddess by her own Pillai caste people.

Muttuvīraṉ - A Powerful Deity

The place where the severed head of Muttuvīraṉ fell was owned by the Tēvars, so they did not allow the Aruntatiyars to worship at that place. The Aruntatiyar community was unable to worship their favourite deity. Due to the power of the brutally murdered Muttuvīraṉ, the agricultural crops cultivated at that place always withered and became fruitless. It was customary for the plowing cows to lie down when they went to plow the land, which was refused worship. Due to this, the owner of the land, had requested the Cakkiliyars to take the deity from there and keep him in another place. The Aruntatiyars refused to do so and the police intervened and helped the Cakkiliyars buy only the necessary space for worship. The Aruntatiyars have been worshipping at this place every year by collecting soil and erecting a mound. During the next year's worship, they worshipped the destroyed and damaged mound by covering it with soil. It is only in recent times that a temple has been built and worshipped at that place instead of a mound. People from towns like Appaṉēri, Ayyaṉēri, Paṭantappuḷi, Tōṇukāl, Citrāmpaṭṭi, Villicēri etc. are beneficiaries of this temple.

Rāmapakaṭai - Ciṉṉanampi

The story of Rāmapakaṭai - Ciṉṉanampi and the story of Ciṉṉanampi which has already appeared in print are basically identical. However, due to the fact that Tirukkuṟuṅkuṭi Nampinātar was born as the son of Pūluṭaiyāl and Ciṉṉanampi is sung as a story of Nampinātar. It is considered a genre of social ballad.

A king from the Aruntatiyar clan named Rāmapakaṭai came to the beautiful area of Vēppilaṅkuḷam near Paṇakuṭi village in Tirunelvēli. After building a great fort, he was worried that he had no children. His wife lamented that she was childless and said that she would visit the temple after fasting for 21 months, hoping that she would be blessed. After worshipping the god Nampi, a child was born to Pūluṭaiyāl. They named him Ciṉṉanampi.

Ciṉṉanampi was sent to a master's house to stay and learn many skills like magic, wrestling, archery, horse riding and elephant riding by the age of sixteen. Being a slave clan, Pūluṭaiyāl came to the village every day to give grass to the unruly horse of Paṇakuṭi Māṇikkavācakam Piḷḷai. As Ciṉṉanampi wanted, his father Rāmapakaṭai went to Cippippāṟai and bought two hunting dogs, Karuvēṅkai and Cevvēṅkai (dog breed). He also used to hunt in Kaḷakkāṭu and Paṇakuṭi Hills.

Ciṉṉanampi, who saw his mother carrying the grass as usual, asked, "Why are you doing this work?" To that, she said, "we are all slave caste, so it is our duty to feed Māṇikkavācakam Piḷḷai's unruly horse." Unbeknownst to her mother, Ciṉṉanampi followed her. After his mother returned home, he untied the unruly horse, brought it out of the stable, rode it round the village, tired it out, tamed the horse and locked it in the stable. On the door of the stable, he wrote, 'The tamer of this horse is Ciṉṉanampi, the son of Rāmapakaṭai of Vēppilaṅkuḷam'. The next morning Māṇikkavācakam Piḷḷai, who was surprised to see this, called Rāmapakaṭai and Pūluṭaiyāl and inquired and praised Ciṉṉanampi and gave him a job as a minister in the palace. He also adopted Ciṉṉanampi as his child.

Māṇikkavācakam Piḷḷai's brother-in-law Tiraviyavācakam Piḷḷai ruled Pāppākkuṭi. His minister Māṭacāmpāṉ was asked to mark the day for ploughing the field. Accordingly, seven pots of potion were tapped when Māṭacāmpāṉ ploughed the field. He told the news to his master. Immediately he called the magician to take the potion. According to him, Tiraviyavācakam Piḷḷai sent a letter to Māṭacāmpāṉ asking for Ciṉṉanampi, the only eldest son of his uncle Māṇikkavācakam Piḷḷai's village in Paṇakuṭi, as there was no one in his village to find and sacrifice his mother's only eldest son. In it, he sent Ciṉṉanampi to his wife for treatment, and on the inner leaf he wrote a message about seven pots of potion. Accordingly, when Māṭacāmpāṉ came, Māṇikkavācakam Piḷḷai was not in town. The wife who read the message became greedy and sent Māṭacāmpāṉ ahead. Later, she summoned Ciṉṉanampi and convinced him with her messy look and hair in a dramatising manner and sent her to get medicine for her sister-in-law.

Thinking this to be true, Ciṉṉanampi, who came to Pāppākkuṭi, gave the leaf that his master had given to Tiraviyavācakam Piḷḷai. He planned with Māṭacāmpāṉ and sent Ciṉṉanampi to go to Māṭacāmpāṉ's house. There, Māṭacāmpāṉ gave a feast and wine to Ciṉṉanampi to deceive him. After that, he said that there was going to be a ritual to their Vayakattu Māṭaṉ (a local deity) and sacrificed Ciṉṉanampi and took the seven pots of potion and carried them in the cart. At that time, the three men (magician, Māṭacāmpāṉ and Tiraviyavācakam Piḷḷai), who were caught in a sudden storm, fell into the river and perished along with seven pots of potion. Ciṉṉanampi's two dogs rolled in his blood and ran to his parents and took them there. The parents picked up the deceased Ciṉṉanampi and stacked logs on the side of the Perumāḷ temple at Pāppākkuṭi. People of that village have built a temple for Ciṉṉanampi in memory of his family.

Ciṉṉakkuruvaṉ - Periyakkūṟuvaṉ

Ciṉṉakkuruvaṉ and Periyakkūṟuvaṉ were the Aruntatiyar warriors who lived in Citrampaṭṭi near Kōvilpaṭṭi. They are chivalrous and good at Cilampam. People who used to beat, kick and knock anyone with a reason would tremble at the sight of them. Therefore, their bravery was also exploited by the Tēvar, Kuṭumpaṉ (Tēvēntirakula Veḷḷāḷar) castes. Ciṉṉakkuruvaṉ and Periyakkūṟuvaṉ had four members of the Tēvar caste and four members of the Kuṭumpaṉ caste as their allies. They had the ability to easily complete the tricks and actions that their partners challenge. Both married and lived happily with their respective wives and children.

They used to rob the rich and help the poor. Thus, they were considered worthy of respect among the people. At the same time they had to earn enemies. There was also an incident in their lives where a person, from the Thevar caste who had a dispute with them, was beaten and burnt to death in the hills of Meyppāṟai.

Even if there is a special event and a marriage between a man and a woman of any caste within the town and in the surrounding villages, it is necessary to give some amount of rice and ten rupees to Ciṉṉakkuruvaṉ and Periyakkūṟuvaṉ and send the information even before the event takes place. If not, they usually beat people coming from the city for marriage and pelt the bus with stones. In addition to this, the farmers have to give them a share in the crop yield. If they did not pay, they would break the 'Kamalai' (a device for drawing water from a well), untie the cows and sell them, and loot the grains. All these activities were done in collaboration with other castes. Along with accomplices, they sometimes used to steal ornaments and money too. Once when a fierce battle between the Aruntatiyars and the Kuṭumpars broke out in the town of Tōṇukāl, Ciṉṉakkuruvaṉ and Periyakkūṟuvaṉ guarded the Aruntatiyars with 50 soldiers for 15 days with swords, machettes, sticks and spears.

Both of them are slender in appearance and of fair height but they had unbelievable courage. Ciṉṉakkuruvaṉ had two sons and a daughter. Ciṉṉakkuruvaṉ was living a happy life with his wife and children. One day, Ciṉṉakkuruvaṉ had gone to a village called Kumāreṭṭiyārpuram for a marriage function. At this time,

Periyakkūṟuvaṉ tried to misbehave with an upper caste girl in the fertile area. The people who were doing work in the area came and beat him up with whatever they got in hand. Periyakkūṟuvaṉ, who went home with internal injuries, drank a cup of water and fell down and died on the spot.

In the past, the upper caste people had a custom of getting married by buying rented clothes and jewellery from Kōvilpaṭṭi. A girl was to get married in the house of a Mēkkāṭṭu Nāyakkar. The family did not give any information to Ciṉṉakkuruvaṉ about the marriage of their daughter. Ciṉṉakkuruvaṉ, who was angry with this idea, planned to fight with them in the wedding house. Knowing this, the Nāyakkars of Cippippāṟai and Meyppāṟai area made a counter plan. Accordingly, they planned to untie the Pantal (ceremonial tent) to trap Ciṉṉakkuruvaṉ. But he ran away with his accomplices. The escapees were lurking on the way of the bridegroom's home, and knowing this, the bride and the groom took that route and came back home. They decided to go back home in the morning. Knowing the trick of the bride and the groom, Ciṉṉakkuruvaṉ sent his allies back. The next day, the Nāyakkars from other towns (Cippippāṟai and Meyppāṟai) had planned to get drunk and to beat Ciṉṉakkuruvaṉ who had come alone. When he went inside his house to get weapons to fight back, the enemies took advantage of this by pelting stones and hitting the lock with a stick and setting the house on fire and left Ciṉṉakkuruvaṉ dead.

Confessions

Whenever the festival is held in commemoration of the killing of Cērvāraṉ, other caste people participate in the prayers in large numbers and celebrate the festival by giving offerings and by receiving blessings. In the agriculturally based villages of Southern district, whenever there is a rain deficit, all the caste people say, "if you worship the Cērvāraṉ Cāmi, offer alms, then the rain will fall and the crops will flourish." This traditional practice continues even today.

The place where Muttuvīraṉ was killed and his head fell was owned by the Tēvars, so they did not allow the Aruntatiyar to worship in that place. Thanks to Muttuvīraṉ's divine power, the agricultural crops cultivated at that place always withered and became useless. The policemen have helped the Cakkiliyar people to buy only the necessary space for worshipping their Cērvāraṉ Cāmi. Many of the older generations who have been benefitted by this temple in towns like Appaṉēri, Ayyaṉēri, Paṭantappuḷi, Tōṇukāl, Citrāmpaṭṭi, Villicēri, and others are given the name 'Muttuvīraṉ'.

After the murder of both Ciṉṉakkuruvaṉ and Periyakkūṟuvaṉ, many people from Citrampaṭṭi village vacated the town and went to other towns in search of livelihood. Ciṉṉakkuruvaṉ and Periyakkūṟuvaṉ are still worshipped by their families by installing a stone in honour of their dead heroes, engraved with their honour in letters, in the house where they died, thinking of both as deities.

Chapter - 8

Kuyili: The Daredevil and Goddess of Fire

Many freedom *fighters* have lived in Tamil Nadu as role models for heroism among Tamils. Among them, women have also become champions. Not only male freedom fighters but also women freedom fighters have sacrificed their lives in the Indian freedom struggle. Rukmini, Durga Devi, Lakṣumipati, Akalyāpāy Kōkālkar, Pīmāpāy, Rani Ceṉṉammā, Kuyili, Vēlunācciyār, Tillaiyāṭi Vaḷḷiyammai, Rātikā Devi, Dr Prabhavati are prominent among them. The history, achievements and sacrifices of some of the women who bravely equaled their men in the Indian War of Independence are recorded and many remain unrecorded. The daredevil Kuyili, an Aruntatiyar woman from Tamil Nadu, was among those whose history is also hidden.

Daredevil Kuyili - A Resurgent Dalit Feminist History

Kuyili was a Dalit woman warrior who took up arms against the British East India Company in the eighteenth century Indian War of Independence. Kuyili was the first Dalit woman to transform herself into a self-sacrificing fighter in the war that took place in present day Tamil Nadu during the Indian freedom struggle. Due to the fact that she was a woman and belonged to the lower caste of Aruntatiyar, Kuyili's role has been left undocumented in the history of the Indian freedom struggle. Finding the social history of oppressed people from written histories is biased. Instead, the recovery of Dalit history with the help of folk ballads can be legitimate and authentic.

Kuyili was the trusted friend of Vēlunācciyār, the queen of Civakaṅkai. She not only became Vēlunācciyār's friend but also her bodyguard and later became a leader of suicide squad to annihilate the British forces. There are some folk and oral stories about her. The pitfalls of obtaining an oral history of Kuyili, a low-caste Aruntatiyar woman, arise because those who know the complete history of Kuyili are from upper caste groups. There is no mention of Kuyili in the inscriptions, palm leaf manuscripts and literature of that time.

During World War II, soldiers committed suicide during the fighting between Germany and Japan. Written history records show that this was the beginning of the Suicide Squad. But not many people know that a Tamil Aruntatiyar woman became the world's first suicide fighter almost a hundred years before the Second World War. As the Tamil woman was a low caste Aruntatiyar, her story has been deliberately hidden from the mainstream history. So it is plausible to assume that those who have recorded history have approached it from a caste perspective. Kuyili's history as an Aruntatiyar woman in a patriarchal society has been deliberately obscured.

Books such as Vēlunācciyār, 2001 by Jeevabharathi, Vēlunācciyār –Viṭutalai Vīrāṅkaṉaiyiṉ Katai, 2008 by Sanmugasundaram, Kuyiliyiṉ Tiyākattil Vēlunācciyāriṉ Veṟṟi, 2013 by Alampattu Ulaganadhan, Chandimao's Kuyili: Rāṇi Vēlunācciyāriṉ Peṇkaḷ Paṭaittaḷapati, 2017 and Ambedkar Priyan's Vīrattāy Kuyili: Āṅkilēyarai Eritta Mutal Taṟkolaip Peṇ Pōrāḷi, 2018 and magazines namely Makaḷir Cintaṉai, November 2010, Aruntamiḻaṉ, May 2010, Āticcam, July-December 2009-10 documented a few important information about Kuyili. On the basis of the above books and pamphlets and on the basis of oral stories received from the people of Sivaganga district, the history and life of Kuyili, the first Dalit woman fighter, is constructed.

Civakaṅkai Cīmai - A Historical background

In the eighteenth century, King Muttu Vaṭukanātar, who ruled the Civakaṅkai region, refused to submit to the oppressions of the English and Nawab of Arcot and fought against them without paying taxes. The British and the Nawab of Arcot conspired to kill Muttu Vaṭukanātar who opposed them. General Joseph Smith (1732-1775) and the British Company forces led by Abraham Bonsor invaded Civakaṅkai. In June 1772, Muttu Vaṭukanātar was martyred in the battle at Kāḷaiyārkōvil. Muttu Vaṭukanātar's second wife Rāṇi Kaurinācciyār was also killed during the battle. Civakaṅkai fort was captured by foreigners. British Company's plot was accomplished by the machinations of his enemies. Muttu Vaṭukanātar's first wife and political successor, Vēlunācciyār, lost her mother and her husband and became isolated. However, Vēlunācciyār decided to recapture the lost region.

After the death of Muttu Vaṭukanātar, Vēlunācciyār, who became the Queen, took a heroic vow that she would not rest until she expelled the Whites from the Civakaṅkai region. For some time she patiently lived in hiding. Hyder Ali, Tipu Sultan and Gopal Nāyakkar, backed Vēlunācciyār. From time to time, Vēlunācciyār consulted with the army commanders about the next battle strategy to recover the Sivaganga region. She decided to divide his forces into three divisions, train them and deploy them in battle. She announced a decisive decision with zeal and intelligence to fight and win against the stranger. That is, 'not only men but also women should be involved in war training'. Many women enthusiastically participated and trained in the war training camp. An eighteen-year-old girl named Kuyili, who was closely attached to the land of her birth and to Vēlunācciyār, also participated in the training camp.

Kuyili's Contribution to Civakaṅkai - Valour and Prudence

Kuyili was born as the daughter of an Aruntatiyar couple named Periyamuttaṉ-Rākku in a village called Kuṭañcāṭi

(Pāsāṇakkarai) near Civakaṅkai. Periyamuttaṉ had immense love for Kuyili who lost her mother in childhood. Muttaṉ showered his love on his daughter and brought up by narrating Vēlunācciyār's heroic glory. Hearing Vēlunācciyār's brave and wise deeds, Kuyili also became a heroic woman. As a result, Kuyili developed great love and loyalty and in time became Queen Vēlunācciyār's favourite warrior. Kuyili was a close friend of the king and a trusted spy. After getting the Queen's support, she learned the martial arts, Cilampam (a weapon-based Indian martial art from Tamil Nadu), horse riding, swordsmanship, etc. from her father. The British resented Kuyili, who was a trusted spy of their enemy, Vēlunācciyār. Kuyili came under the watchful eye of the British. The British also planned to kill Kuyili.

Cilampam Instructor - Betrayal of Kuyili's Guru

Vēlunācciyār's guardian and guru Veṟṟivēl Tēvar alias Cilampu Vāttiyār tricked Kuyili into paying her and asking her to hand over a secret letter to Mallāri Rāyaṉ, who lived in a house near Civakaṅkai Palace. Suspicious of her master's actions and words, Kuyili read the letter he had given him without anyone knowing. The following is the letter written by Mallāri Rāyaṉ's trusted friend Cilampu Vāttiyār : "Dear Mallāri Rāyaṉ, Somehow Vēluṇācciyār got to know about the secret relationship between you and me. She decided that many secret messages would go through me to the King and Nawab of Putukkōṭṭai. Maharani now looks at me suspiciously. I think there may have been mistrust in me. So tell all our people not to have any contact with me for a while!. Let's postpone our communication and contact for a while."

With regards,

Veṟṟivēl - Cilampu Vāttiyār

Kuyili, who is so loyal to Vēlunācciyār, after having read the letter which was written by Veṟṟivēl Tēvar, got terribly annoyed. Kuyili stabbed Veṟṟivēl Tēvar to pieces with a knife who wanted to betray the one who was loyal to him. Vēlunācciyār hugged and consoled Kuyili who fell at the queen's feet and cried for killing her guru. Later, Kuyili is approached from the point of view of being the killer of Veṟṟivēl Tēvar alias Cilampu Vāttiyār, who betrayed Vēlunācciyār despite becoming a suicide fighter to save Civakaṅkai region.

Communal Riots - Mallāri Rāyaṉ's Conspiracy

The death of the traitor Veṟṟivēl Tēvar was a great blow to the British. Some people tried to castigate Kuyili's actions by giving it a communal twist. Wanting to gain the goodwill of the British, Mallari Rayan hatched a conspiracy to turn the death of Veṟṟivēl into a 'communal riot'.

Mallari Rayan spread the false propaganda among the people of Civakaṅkai that Vēlunācciyār killed the upper caste Veṟṟivēl Tēvar through a low caste woman. He informed the villages around Civakaṅkai by beating tom-tom and gathered the people together. Due to this, casteism was fuelled in Civakaṅkai region and the huts of the downtrodden people were set on fire. Tension gripped the local areas around Civakaṅkai. Chandimao writes this as follows: "A justification was needed to rally people against Kuyili and Vēlunācciyār. That is caste. What is the justification for punishing our upper caste soldiers with scheduled castes? That fuelled caste hatred. The plot did not gain acceptance among the people of the region. The enraged thugs gathered a crowd and caused violence in Civakaṅkai and every village where the scheduled caste people live. Livestock, agricultural lands and houses were burnt. Assets built up over generations were destroyed. Most of the Scheduled Caste people have shifted their residences to other places." (2017:23-24).

Knowing this, Vēlunācciyār keeps Kuyili under her protection, thinking that she will be in danger at any time. From that day Kuyili was appointed as Vēlunācciyār's bodyguard. Kuyili felt proud and secure about it. She considered it an opportunity to protect and serve the Rani closely. But the upper caste folks could not tolerate the growing influence of Kuyili in the Queen's palace.

One night when she was staying with Queen Vēlunācciyār, a knife suddenly flew towards Vēlunācciyār who was sleeping. Kuyili seized it and saved the Queen's life. From that day Kuyili became the permanent star of hope for the Queen. Kuyili, who was the Queen's bodyguard until then, was appointed as the commander of Vēlunācciyār's women's corps. The Queen named the force as 'Uṭaiyāḷ's Army'.

Caste Hatred - Vēlunācciyār's Sensational Public Declaration

Considering the frequent threats to her life, caste hatred and tension among the people, Vēlunācciyār issued a public announcement to her soldiers as a precautionary measure. "Enemies have come from Sivaganga soil to our residence in Viruppācci and threw knives in my room where I was sleeping. Is this to kill me? Or to kill Kuyili? That's all right. But how did they come so boldly into my room? That is my question. They would not have achieved this feat without the support of our soldiers. I believe that the weapon called caste which our enemies have taken to defeat me at last in Civakaṅkai has also affected our soldiers. Cilampu Vāttiyār, who had received all my favours and rewards, betrayed me. But Kuyili, who did not take any favours, saved my life. Even though Cilampu Vāttiyār was my own caste member, he committed treachery. But, even though Kuyili was born in the Cakkiliyar clan, hasn't she identified and weeded out those who betrayed our country?. If caste is important to you, you can leave my army right now. I don't need casteists," (K. Jakkaiyyan, 2012: 4-5) thus, angrily announced. The soldiers and the public accepted it as it was, considering the justice of this announcement issued by the Queen based on the controversy over the caste of Kuyili.

The day after the pubertal ritual of Vēlunācciyār's daughter Veḷḷacci, the whites abduct her. A division led by Periya Marutu, a division led by Ciṉṉa Marutu and a third division led by Kuyili were engaged in a search operation to rescue Veḷḷacci. Queen herself led the fourth division and started a search expedition.

Kuyili chased the white man on her horse, who had tied Veḷḷacci to a horse and kidnapped her. A fierce battle broke out between the British forces and the Vēlunācciyār forces in Pirāṉmalai forest area. Vēlunācciyār and Kuyili surrounded the enemies who were trying to escape. Kuyili cut off the white man's right hand when he tried to shoot Vēlunācciyār with his gun to escape danger. Vēlunācciyār cut off the head of the white man who had kidnapped her daughter and chopped him into pieces. Vēlunācciyār's forces were fierce in the final battle to fully recover control of Civakaṅkai from the Whites.

The first woman suicide fighter of the Indian Independence War

The Whites stockpiled ammunition and arms near Civakaṅkai Palace to defeat Vēlunācciyār. Even though the Vēlunācciyār army had valiant warriors, it did not have any sophisticated and powerful weapons like the British had. A situation arose where the war could not be won without destroying the British arsenal. Kuyili, the Queen's bodyguard, who knew well that discipline is also needed in war training, without waiting for the queen's order, poured boiling ghee on her body, climbed the palace wall, jumped into the British armoury and detonated it. The armoury was completely destroyed by fire. This event is chronicled by Periyaṇṇaṉ which was narrated by Marutāyi, one of the women commanders of Vēlunācciyār. "Empress! When the battle started Kuyili quickly ran into the temple. I also went behind to see her. She poured the boiling ghee all over her body which was kept for lighting lamps in the temple. She took the fire bond from the temple and went to the upper part of the palace. From there she set fire to her body and jumped into the pile of British weapons. Kuyili laid down her life and set fire to the weapons of Britishers." (1997:150). This message is recorded in the oral songs.

'Daredevil Kuyili
Saved the life of
The Queen (Vēlunācciyār)

By jumping into those dangerous
Britishers' armoury', sings Kollaṅkuṭi Karuppāyi Ammāḷ
'Applying ghee all over her body
Throwing the burning lamp
Into the British armoury
Kuyili jumped into it'

This is the folk song that Chandimao has written in his book that village singer Ciṅkampuṇari taṅkarācu sang a few years ago. With this, Kuyili became the first suicide Dalit woman fighter of the Indian Independence War.

Kuyili's Sacrifice: Vēlunācciyār's Victory

Kuyili, the daredevil, a Dalit woman who became a suicide warrior for the victory of Vēlunācciyār, is hailed as the champion of Civakaṅkai Cīmai. Kuyili's bravery and wisdom, which led to the victory of Vēlunācciyār through her self-sacrifice, is a source of pride not only for the Aruntatiyar community but also for other communities across the nation.

Goddess of Fire: Constructing through Oral History

Goddesses who descended into fire pits for prayer and women who took their lives by leaping into the fire were called 'Mālai Teyvaṅkaḷ' (those who have attained the status of god by diving into fire), who were devotees of such deities. After the death of their husbands, the wives who had no desire to live in this world were called 'Tīppāñca Ammaṉ' (goddess of fire). Social history refers to this as 'Sati', which means women burn themselves alive on the funeral pyre of husband. In this way, the dead are worshipped as family deities.

Aruntatiyar Kuyili, who poured boiling ghee on her body and took her own life by jumping into the armoury of the British to save her country, was completely different from other gods and goddesses.

Kuyili Memorial

A memorial pillar to Kuyili has been installed in Civakaṅkai Vēlunācciyār Memorial Hall. The heroic exploits and sacrifices of Kuyili are written in the inscription on the statue of Queen Vēlunācciyār located in front of the Civakaṅkai Palace. Descendants of Kuyili have a tradition of paying respects to Kuyili's memorial pillar on Vijayatacami day every year.

According to the oral history of the people living in that place, there is a memorial to Kuyili in the village of Poṉṉaṅkuḷam near Civakaṅkai and there is a temple called 'Goddess of Fire' in Muttuppaṭṭi village in memory of Kuyili.

Ambedkar Priyan writes, "A virgin girl who had set fire to the palace was buried at this place, and the people of the village thought of her as the goddess and gave the goddess the name 'Goddess of Fire' to the goddess (*2018:*140).

'மாகாளி பூவாயி //Mākāḷi Pūvāyi//
சிலம்பாயி ஆத்தா //Cilampāyi Āttā//
முத்துப்பட்டி ஊருக்குள்ள //Muttuppaṭṭi Ūrukkuḷḷa//
மொனமுறியா மஞ்ச அவ //Moṉamuṟiyā Mañca Ava//
சமஞ்சு நின்னா பூத்து //Camañcu Niṉṉā Pūttu//
குயிலி எனும் நாத்து' //Kuyili Eṉum Nāttu//[1]

This is how the people of Muttuppaṭṭi village worship by singing Muḷaippāri (small pottery filled with nine types of sprouted grains) song.

Political Rights

There is a twist that Kuyili is a fictional character in Vēlunācciyār's history of success and that Kuyili is Vēlunācciyār's adopted daughter. Some claim that Kuyili belongs to the 'Cāmpavar' clan of Paṟaiyar community of Tamil Nadu.

1. This folk song describes, in short, describes Kuyili's pubertal stage.

A 'Kuyili Ammaṉ temple' was found in Vaḷḷiyammāḷpuram in Ālaṅkuḷam taluka of Tirunelvēli district during the field survey. It is additional news that the worshippers of this temple are Aruntatiyars. It is certain that the people who worship Kuyili as a goddess are the Aruntatiyars.

Apart from Aruntatiyar, the practice of building a temple and worshipping Kuyili is not known to exist among other communities in Tamil Nadu. It is also noteworthy here that there are several women with the name 'Kuyili' among the Aruntatiyar people in Civakaṅkai district. The practice of naming 'Kuyili' is not found among other communities in Tamil Nadu. Oral histories found during fieldwork conducted in villages of Civakaṅkai district suggest that Kuyili belonged to the Aruntatiyar community. It is worth recalling here that Prof Suba Veerapandiyan has stated in one of his interviews that Kuyili is an Aruntatiyar woman. The same point was reiterated by Tiruchy Siva in the Indian Parliament (June, 2021). With this, it is clearly seen that Kuyili, who is known as the first female suicide bomber in the Indian Independence War, belonged to the Aruntatiyar community.

References

Sources in Tamil:

1. Arunan, 2006. *Kolaikkaḷaṅkaḷiṉ vākkumūlam*, Madurai, Vasantham Veliyittagam
2. Arunachalam.M. 1969. *Caiva Camayam*, Madurai: Meenakshi Puthaka Nilaiyam.
3. Appadurai, Ka. 1971. *Teṉṉāṭṭup pōrkkaḷaṅkaḷ*, Chennai: Pari Nilaiyam.
4. Ambedkar Piriyan, C. 2018. *Vīrattāy Kuyili: Āṅkilēyarai Eritta Mutal Taṟkolaip Peṇ Pōrāḷi,* Chennai: Ulakath Tamilaraycci Niruvanam.
5. Anbuselvam. 2016. *Āṣhe Paṭukolai: Mīḷum Talit Vicāraṇai*, Chennai: Pulam Veliyitu.
6. Anandakumar, M. *'Tirunelvēli Māvaṭṭattil Kuṭiyamarnta Cem'māṉ Makkaḷiṉ Iṉavaraiviyal'* Puthu Visai, December, 2013, pp. 55-57.
7. Anantharasan, J, 2002. *Pavuttamum Paḻantamiḻk Kuṭimakkaḷum,* Chennai: Anrril Pathippagam.
8. Basil Xavier. 2010. *Tamiḻaka Aṭaiyāḷa Araciyaliṉ Pariṇāma Vaḷarcci: Aruntatiyar Aṭaiyāḷa Uruvākkam,* A. Jeganathan & L. Jeyachanthiran (Edrs.), Article in the book of Aṭaiyāḷa Uruvākkamum Aṭaiyāḷa Vēṟupāṭu, Madurai Gurunanak Aayvu pp. 159-163.
9. Bhaktavatchala Bharathi, 2002. *Tamiḻar Māṉiṭaviyal*, Chithambaram: Meyyappaṉ Thamilayvakam.
10. Balachandran, R, B. Dhanancheyan (Edrs.). 2008. *Tamiḻk Kataippāṭalkaḷ*, New Delhi: Sahitya Akademi.
11. Caldwell, 2004. (InTamil: N. Sanjeevi & Krishna Sanjeevi). *Tirunelvēli Carittiram*, Chennai: Kavya.
12. Dayalan, P. *Viṭutalai Puraṭciyiṉ Vīrāṅkaṇai Durkā Dēvi,* Kirru, 16.01.204.
13. Dhananjeyan, A. 2006. *Viḷimpunilai Makkaḷ Vaḻakkāṟukaḷ Iṉavaraiviyal āyvu*, Puducheery: Meyyappan Pathippagam.
14. Gnanathai, M. 2006: *Maṟavar Kataippāṭalkaḷ*, Chennai, Kavya.
15. Gurugudasa Pillai, S. 2012. *Tirunelvēli Cīmai Carittiram,* Chennai: Kavya.
16. Iḷangovan Ezhil. 2002. *Aruntatiyar Varalāṟum Paṇpāṭum*, Coimbatore: Athithamizhar Peravai.
17. ----------------, 1995. *17-Ām nūṟṟāṇṭil Aruntatiyar*, Chennai: Vinthan Veliyeedu.
18. ----------------, 1996. *Mātiyappāvai*, (Pāvai-1), Chennai: Vinthan Veleedu
19. ----------------, 2003. *Maduraivīraṉ Kolaiyum Tirumalai Nāyakkar Makāluṃ*, Coimbatore.

20. ----------------, 2008. *Aruntatiyar Iyakka Varalāṟu*, Chennai: Kalakam Veliyeedu. Athithamizhar Peravai Veliyeedu.
21. ----------------, 2010. *Māvīrar Oṇṭivīraṉ Pakaṭai*, Coimbatore: Athithamizhar Peravai.
22. Jakkaiyan, K. 2011. *Oppilla Viṭutalaip Porali Oṇṭivīraṉ*, Samookaneethi Thamizh Desam, January, 2011.
23. ----------------, 2012. *Intiya Viṭutalaip Pōriṉ Iṇaiyaṟṟa Pōrāḷikaḷ*, Keetru, 21 Aguest, 2012.
24. Jeevabharathi, K. 2001. *'Vēlu Nācciyār' (Varalāṟṟup Putiṉam),* Chennai: Vairam Veliyeedu.
25. Jeyaveeradevan, S. 2010. *Ceruppu- Oru Varalāṟṟup Pārvai*, Paavai Publications.
26. Kanmani, M.S. *Kuyili: Taṟkoṭaitāri*, Aathicham, July-December, 2009-2010, pp. 21, 35, 49, 51, 78 & 100, Karaikkudi: Alakappa Palkalaikkazhagam.
27. Kandasamy Pulavar, Muthalankurichi, 1948. *Tiruccentūr Noṇṭi Nādakam*, Tiruchentur: Sri Suppiramaniyaswami Devastanam Veliyitu-2.
28. Kasinathan, Nadana, 2011. *Teṉpakutip Pāḷaiyakkārarkaḷ Varalāṟu,* Chennai: Manivasakar Patippagam.
29. Krishnamurthy, M.A., 2010, *Aruntatiyar Camūkattiṉ Ariya Varalāṟu,* Chennai: Kavya.
30. Magarasan, 2006. *Kīḻiruntu Eḻukiṉṟa Varalāṟu*, Chennai: Parisal.
31. Manikandan, R. 2012. *Vīram Viḷainta Tamiḻ Pūmi'*, Chennai: Kumutham, Pu (tu) ttagam Veliyeetu.
32. Mathivannan, M, 2012, *Aṟiñarkaḷiṉ Puraḷiyum Aruntatiyar Varalāṟum*, Vellaik Kuthirai (July-Aguest, 2012), Kovai.
33. ----------------, 2008. *Aruntatiyarkaḷākiya Nāṅkaḷ*, Chennai: Karuppu Piratikaḷ.
34. ----------------, 2007. *Uḷ otukkīṭu: Cila Pārvaikaḷ*, Chennai: Karuppu Piratikaḷ.
35. Mayilvakanan Gurusamy. 2018. *Oppaṉaikaḷiṉ Kūttu (Civakaṅkai Varalāṟṟai Muṉvaittu ōr āyvu),* Chennai: Neendhum Meenkal Veliyeettakam.
36. Manokaran Somarasa. 2015. *Vīrattirumakaḷ Mūvar*, Civapuram Intu Cikāmaṇi (September, 2015), Chennai.
37. Mariappan, A. 2002. *Tēciyamum Tamiḻ Ilakkiyamum*, Chennai: Kavya.
38. Maṟc, 2001. *Aruntatiyar: Vāḻum Varalāṟu*, Palayamkottai: Nattar Vaḻakkaṟṟiyal Aayvu Maiyam.
39. Muthalankurichi Kamarasu, 2012. *Teṉpāṇṭic Cīmaiyilē*, Chennai: Kavya.
40. ----------------, 2013. *'Nellai Jamīṉkaḷ: Camastāṉaṅkaḷum Carivukaḷum'*, Chennai: Vikatan piracuram.
41. ----------------, 2017. 'Ciṅkampaṭṭi Camīṉ Catai' Chennai: Kavya.
42. Muthiah, I. 2008. *'Nāṭṭuppuṟak Kataippāṭalum Varalāṟṟu Varaiviyal Kaṭṭaviḻppum'*, Balachandiran. Irā. Ā. Dhananjeyan (Edr.), Tamiḻk Kataippāṭalkaḷ Nūliluḷḷa Kaṭṭurai, pp. 80-102. New Delhi: Sakitya Academy.
43. Murugan, R, 2004. *Caṅkap Pākkaḷil Tolkuṭik Kūṟukaḷ*, Puduchery: Anandhai veliyitu.
44. Murugesan, C.S., 2009. *'Teṉṉintiyak Kōṭṭaikaḷ'* Chennai: Asokan pathippakam.
45. Muthukirishnan, A. 2008. *Malattil Tōynta Māṉuṭam*, Chennai: Uyirmai Veḷiyeetu.
46. *Nakkeeran*, Vaara Ithal, Janaury, 29, 2002.
47. Natarajan, M, 2005. *Toṭṭiya Nāyakkar Kulateyva Vaḻipāṭu*, Unpublished Ph.D Thesis, Periyar University.

48. -----------------, 2003. *Paṉpāṭṭu Māṉiṭaviyal*. Chithambaram. Meyyappan Pathippagam.

49. Panneerselvam, V. 2006. *Aravākkuṟicci Vaṭṭāra Aruntatiyar Iṉa Makkaḷin Avarkaḷiṉ Kulateyvak Kōvilkaḷum: Ōr āyvu,* Unpublished Ph.D Thesis, Bharathiyar University.

50. -----------------, 2008. *Aruntatiyar yār? - Oru Varalāṟṟup Pārvai,* Coimbatore: Vaikai Patippagam.

51. Pandian, M.S., *Bārata Viṭutalaip Pōril Tamiḻakam*, Nagercoil: Anpu Nilaiyam, Vadiveespuram.

52. Pandian, Neela. *Tīppāyntammaṉ Vaḻipāṭu: Poṭṭippuram Cīlaikkāri Ammaṉ*, Kaavya Tamiḻ, January - March, 2019, pp. 31-36.

53. Periyannan, K. 1997. *Teṉtamiḻakam Tanta Tiyāka Tīpaṅkaḷ*, Chennai: Vanathi Patippagam.

54. Perumal. A.K. 2003. *'Teyvaṅkaḷ Muḷaikkum Nilam'*, Chennai: Tamizhini.

55. Ragupathi, Ko. 2008. *Tīṇṭappaṭātavarkaḷiṉ Tīṇṭappaṭṭa Aṟiviyal Toḻil Nutpam*, pp. 8-15. Puthuvisai, April-June, 2008).

56. Ramasamy, A. 2009. Ravikumar, *Mīḷum Varalāṟu: Aṟiyappaṭāta Nantaṉiṉ Kaṭai Nūlukku Eḻutiya Matippurai,* Chennai: IITS.

57. Rasaiya, N. 1990. *Intiya Viṭutalaip Pōril Tāḻttappaṭṭōriṉ Paṅku*, Ayyan Kollan Kondan: Gnanamurugan Eluttakam.

58. -----------------, 2005. *Pūlittēvaṉ Cintu*, Ayyan Kollan Kondan: Gnanamurugan eluttagam.

59. Rajayyan, K. 2012. (In Tamil: Neyvēli Balu). *'Tamiḻnāṭṭup Pāḷaiyakkārarkaḷiṉ Tōṟṟamum Vīḻcciyum',* Madurai: Karuttu Pattarai.

60. Rasu, S, (Edr.) 1991. *Koṅku Nāṭṭuc Camutāya āvaṇaṅkaḷ,* Thanjavur: Tamil Palkalaik Kalakam.

61. Rasaiah, N. 2005. *Pūlittēvaṉ Cintu*, Ayankollan Kondan: Gnanamurukan Eluthagam.

62. -----------------, 1990. *Viṭutalaip Pōril Tāḻttappaṭṭōriṉ Paṅku,* Ayankollan Kondan, Gnanamurukan Eluthagam.

63. Sakthivel, S. 2007. *Tirunelvēli Māvaṭṭa Nāṭṭuppuṟaviyal Aḷavāyvu,* Thanjavur: Tamilp Palkalaikkazhaga Veliyeedu.

64. Sanmugasundaram, S. 2011. *Nellai Nāṭṭuppuṟa Teyvaṅkaḷ: Vaḻipāṭum Paṉpāṭum*, Chennai: Kavya.

65. -----------------, 2008. *Vēlunācciyār- Viṭutalai Vēṅkaiyiṉ Katai*, Chennai: Kavya.

66. Sanmugasundaram Kaavya. (Edr.) 2007. Māvīraṉ Pūlittēvaṉ, Chennai: Kavya.

67. Sanmugaṉ, S. Kodumudi, 1994. *Paḻantamiḻar Poṟiyiyal Nutpaṅkaḷ- Part-I,* Chennai: Meengopal Pathippakam.

68. Sathurvethi Sathathanar, 2019. *Vaciṣta Vamcam*, Karamadai: Sri Arunthathi Pothunala Arakkattaḷai.

69. -----------------, 1981. *Cēlam Māvaṭṭattu Naṭukaṟkaḷ*, Tenolai, April, 1981.

70. Santhimavo, 2017. *Kuyili: Irāṇi Vēlunācciyāriṉ Peṇkaḷ Paṭaittaḷapati*, Vathalakundu: Oviya Pathippagam.

71. Sampath, P. 2007. *Nāṅkaḷ Varukiṟōm: Aruntatiyar Vāḻvum Viṭutalaiyum*, Chennai: Bharathi Puthakalayam.

72. Saravanan, N. 2019. *Talittiṉ kuṟippukaḷ*, Chennai: Elini patippagam.

73. -----------------, 2008. Viṭiyalai nōkki aruntatiyar, Chennai: Bharathi Puthaklayam.

74. Saravanaṉ, P. 2014. *Intiya Cutantirap Pōrāṭṭa Vīrarkaḷ*, Chennai: Kilakku Pathippagam.
75. *Sākkiyar Kural*, November-1- 2010, Malar-1, Itaḻ-1. Selam: Sakkiyar Arakkattalai.
76. Sami, R.P., 2009. *Maṉitaṉ Cumanta Varuṇak Koṭumaikaḷ*, Bangalore: Lakshmi Villa.
77. Sami, V.N. 2003. *Intiya Viṭutalaikku Iṉṉuyir īnta Vīrāṅkaṉaikaḷ*, Chennai: Sri Hindu Publications.
78. Sivasubramanian, A. 2009. *Iṉavaraiviyalum Tamiḻ Nāvalum*, Chennai: Parisal.
79. -----------------, *Paṭittup Pāruṅkaḷēṉ', Amarāvati: Varalāṟu, Tolliyal, Kalveṭṭu, Nāṇayaviyal Nūl Kuṟitta Kaṭṭurai*, Ungal Noolagam, September 2017, pp. 4-9.
80. ------------------. 2010. *Aṭittaḷa Makkaḷ Varalāṟu*, Chennai: New Century Book House Pvt.
81. Seenivasan, P., 2004. *Tīṇṭāmaikkut Tīyiṭu*, Chidambaram: Mangai pathippagam.
82. Seenivasan, S., Ponraj, V., (Edrs.) 2010, *Dalit Kataippāṭalkaḷ (Teṉ Māvaṭṭaṅkaḷ),* Chennai: Kavya.
83. Seenivasan, S., 2016. *Cērvāraṉ Cāmi: Varalāṟum Kataippāṭalum,* Araichipatti: Kanchi Pathippagam.
84. Senrayapperumal, P. 2012. *Rājārāṇi āṭṭa āṟṟukai Muṟaikaḷum Ataṉ Camūka Nilaikaḷum*, Unpublished Ph.D Thesis, Madurai Kamarajar University.
85. Sridhar, T. Sri. (Edr.). 2009. *Tirunelvēli Māvaṭṭak Kalveṭṭukaḷ*, Chennai: Tamil Nadu Thholliyal Thurai.
86. Suganti Annathai, A. *Tolliyal Nōkkil Pūlittēvaṉ Varalāṟu* Tamiḻmoḻi Maṟṟum Ilakkiya Paṉṉāṭṭu āyvitaḻ, April, 2019.
87. Tamilnila. *Civakaṅkaiyai Mīṭṭa Taṟkolaip Paṭai Tākkutal*, Dinakaran-vasantam, 18.08.2013, Pak.22-23.
88. Thurston, Edgar. (In Tamil Ka. Rathinam) 2005, *Teṉṉintiyak Kulaṅkaḷum Kuṭikaḷum - 2*, Tanjavur: Tamil Palkalaikkazhagam.
89. -----------------. (InTamil Ka. Rathinam), 2003 (1975). *Teṉṉintiyak Kulaṅkaḷum Kuṭikaḷum -5,* Tanjavur: Tamil Palkalaikkazhagam.
90. Ulakanathan. Alampattu, S. 2013. *Kuyiliyiṉ Tiyākattil Vēlunācciyāriṉ Veṟṟi,*
91. *Uḻaippavar āyutam,* Janauary -2010, Thiruvannamalai.
92. Vargees Jeyaraj, S. 2009. (In Tamil: Yusuf Raja). *'Tamiḻnāṭṭil Jamīṉtāri Mūṟai: Maturai māvaṭṭam'*, Chennai: Pavai Publications.
93. Vaigai Anees, 2014. *'Aḻinta Jamīṉkaḷum Aḻiyāta Kalveṭṭukaḷum'*, Devathanappatti: Akamatu Nisma Publications.

Sources in English:

1. Amudha, M.V., *Kuyili: The Dalit Commander whose sacrifice remains unsung tale*, Indian women in history, July, 31.2018.
2. Basil Xavier, S. 2020. *Ethnophilophising in India; A Study on Arunthathiyars*, New Delhi: Authors Press.
3. Berreman Gerald, D. 1968. *Ethnography: Method and Product,* In James A. Clifton (Ed.) Introduction to Cultural Anthropology: Essays in the scope and methods of Man, pp. 337-373. Boston: Houghton Mifflin Company.
4. Deliège, Robert, 1993. *The Myths of origin of the Indian Untouchables*, Man (NS) 28:533-549.

5. Dumont, Louis (Translated from French by M. Moffatt, L, and A. Morton), 1986, *A South Indian sub-caste: Social organization and religion of the Piramalai Kallar*, Delhi; Oxford University Press.
6. Ekta Singh, 2009. *Caste system in India: A Historical Perspective*, Delhi: Kalpaz Publications.
7. Fawcett, 1903. *Kondaiamkottai Maravars: A Dravidian Tribe of Tinnevelly, South India*, Journal of the Royal Anthropological Institute, 33:57-68.
8. Joganand, P.G., 1995. *Dalit Women: Issues and Perspectives*, Pune: Gyan Publishing House.
9. Kangasabai, V., 1989. *The Tamils Eighteen Hundred Years ago*, New Delhi: Asian Educational Services.
10. Krishnamoorthy, A., 2017. *Arunthathiyar: The Great Leather Workers of Tamil Nadu - Life & History*, Chennai: Nagalagam Publication.
11. Manikandan, S., 2013. *'Contest for Power and Legitimacy; Little Kingdoms of Southern Tamil Country during the Eighteenth Century'* unpublished Ph D thesis, Department of History, School of Social Sciences and International Studies, Pondicherry University.
12. Meena Anand (Ed.), 2011. *Dalit Women: Fear and Discrimination*, Delhi: Isha Books.
13. Moffat, Michael, 1979. *An Untouchable Community in South India: Structure and Consensus*, Princeton, New Jersey: Princeton University Press.
14. Naik, C.D., 2010. *Buddhism and Dalits: Social Philosophy and Traditions*, Delhi: Kalpaz Publications.
15. Naimishray Mohan Dass, 2010. *Dalit Freedom Fighters*, New Delhi: Gyan Publishing House.
16. Pandian, T.B., 1893. *The Slaves of the Soil in South India*, Madras: The Cosmopolite Press.
17. Pillai, K.K, 1979. *The Caste system of Tamil Nadu*, Chennai: MJP Publisher.
18. Thurston, Edger, 1975. *Ethnographic Notes in Southern India, Part-II*, Delhi: Cosmo Publications.
19. Vanamaamalai, N., 1981. *Interpretation of Tamil Folk Creations*, Trivandrum, Dravidian Linguistics Association.
20. Venkata Siva Reddy, G., 2002. *'Ghanshyam Competitions and Conflict among Dalits: Madiga Dandora Movement in Andhra Pradesh'* in Shah's (Ed.) Dalits and the State, Mussoorie: Centre for Rural Studies, LBSNAA.
21. Young, Michael W., 1979. *The Ethnography of Malinowski: The Trobriand Islands 1915 -1918,* London: Routledge & Kegan Paul Ltd.
22. Zelliot Eleanor, 1998. *From Untouchable to Dalit*, New Delhi: Manohar Publishers & Distributers
23. https://en.wikipedia.org/wiki/Kuyili
24. https://en.wikipedia.org/wiki/Velu_Nachiyar

Index